"Victoria's heart for encouraging moms is apparent in every word of this book. The practical steps and insightful reflection questions included in each chapter offer moms the tangible action points they need in order to thrive as mothers. I have no doubt that this book will prove helpful to every mom who reads it, in every stage of her motherhood journey."

STACEY MORGAN, author of *The Astronaut's Wife*

"Every mom should have this book! Victoria Riollano does a fantastic job of addressing the underlying insecurities that mothers may face and how God can empower them to be the best version of themselves for their families. She outlines in a clear way the role and purpose that God has for mothers of all walks of life. This is a handbook of how to live victoriously by relying on the power of God in the day-to-day activities of being a wife and mother."

KEVIN BORDEAUX, lead pastor and founder of Thrive Church, Richmond, VA

"In a tug-of-war world that demands mothers either bend to cultural standards or meet an impossible list of religious prerequisites, Victoria reminds us that rearing children for God's kingdom can be beautiful but messy, bold yet scary, and that amid the humanity of motherhood's demands, God smiles and says, 'I made that mama a warrior. Look at her go!'"

PEYTON GARLAND, author of *Tired, Hungry, & Kinda Faithful* and *Not So by Myself*

"As a pastor, I talk to a lot of moms that just don't feel like they have the knowledge and skills needed to raise their children. They struggle with confidence, past mistakes, and society's expectations. But I've found that most mothers just want to make sure they raise their children to love the Lord. *Warrior Mother* is a great book to help you with that. This book will give you the confidence you need to make the uncomfortable decisions to ensure your family will live according to the Word of God."

JOE RIOLLANO, pastor at Enlighten Church, Stafford, VA

"Many mothers desire a guidebook, a playbook even, to help them navigate the often strange yet wonderful journey of motherhood. When I realized that such a perfect book only existed in my dreams, I did the next best thing—I turned to my trusted community of friends and family who were either a few steps or miles ahead of me and gleaned as much encouragement and wisdom from them as I could. Although every mother's journey is different, there is something life-giving about sharing our stories with and for each other.

In *Warrior Mother*, Victoria does just that. Readers will not only be able to learn effective strategies from her motherhood story, but they will also be able see themselves in it. With faith-filled tools, Victoria reminds mothers of their God-given identity and purpose and provides examples of how to wield their weapons of warfare for the good of their families and legacies. I am excited for mothers to get this timely resource into their hands and hearts."

QUANTRILLA ARD, PhD, author, speaker, blogger at The PhD Mamma, grief coach, and host of *It's All Grief to Me* podcast

WARRIOR MOTHER

Equipping Your Heart to Fight for Your Family's Faith

Victoria Riollano

Foreword by Quantrilla Ard, PhD

KREGEL
PUBLICATIONS

Cataloging-in-Publication Data is available from the Library of Congress.

ISBN 978-0-8254-4768-6, print
ISBN 978-0-8254-7010-3, epub
ISBN 978-0-8254-7109-4, Kindle

Printed in the United States of America
23 24 25 26 27 28 29 30 31 32 / 5 4 3 2 1

This book is dedicated to my children,
Trinity, Joseph, Christian, Isaiah, David, Heavenly Joy,
and Malachi.
You are my greatest accomplishment.
It's a privilege to serve as your mother.
You are deeply loved.

Children are a heritage from the LORD, *offspring*
a reward from him.
Psalm 127:3

Contents

Foreword

I'VE ALWAYS WANTED TO BE a mother. From the moment I cradled my son's diminutive form in my arms, a surge of holy awe mixed with sheer terror filled my swollen body. I instinctively ached to protect him from the dangers of the world—the shadowy *isms* that marked my journey to adulthood. Many nights I've prayed with and for all my children, petitioning God to keep them safe, keep them healthy, make them kind, and the list goes on and on. But I often found myself anxious about their growth and development despite my faith in God and prayers to Him, making me question whether I was *doing* motherhood correctly.

Somewhere deep inside I knew there were no perfect mothers, only mothers who consistently submitted themselves and their parenting to the Lord. Yet my struggle with maternal perfectionism was formidable, combined with other battles that presented themselves daily. As my children grew, I decided to fight effectively and with fervent tenacity. I had to become a warrior for them and for myself. There was no manual for this, and with the steady ache in my heart from the absence of my own mother, the learning curve was and still is steep. But I've seen the results of the shift in my home, and I continue to persevere.

The Christian mother faces tough challenges as she parents in a world that lauds instant gratification over patience, quick fixes over sustainable solutions, and general apathy toward spiritual things. It is easy to become frustrated and exhausted putting out so many little fires while trying to maintain some semblance of peace and structure in the home.

Rather than being a loving and caring example of God to her children, a mother can become hardened by the very responsibility given to her by her Creator. This is where the Enemy of our souls seeks to edge in and unravel the thread of family.

But no longer. Every mother needs tools in her arsenal to support her in one of the most gut-wrenchingly beautiful journeys in her life—raising her children. This book is one of them. When Victoria graciously allowed me to read through its pages, I laughed, I cried, and I found freedom in my mothering. I also felt the profound urge to find a suit of armor and keep it in my closet for a boost every now and then. But I digress.

Warrior Mother: Equipping Your Heart to Fight for Your Family's Faith is a precious, hard-won, battle-tested companion for Christian mothers who seek to stand in their God-given authority. To every mother who desires to intentionally close the gaps and place boundaries around and within her child's heart to overcome the Enemy's snares, this book is for you.

Victoria is uniquely positioned to share these truths with mothers from her own motherhood journey and faith in God. She speaks and writes with the heart of a warrior who has, with the help she has so thoughtfully provided in this book, found her footing. I have watched her implement these strategies in her family over the years as she has prayed and fasted and spoken truth over her children with confidence and expectancy in the God who empowers all mothers to do the same.

There will always be battles to fight, and we get to teach and model for our children how to do so valiantly. Victoria comes alongside readers, gives them practical wisdom, and highlights the spiritual and psychological aspects of their impact as mothers. She doesn't suggest that these strategies are a one-and-done fixer-upper type of to-do list but that these strategies are a lifestyle and are to be utilized consistently. *Warrior Mother* will be a blessing to every mother in whose hands it lands and to the children who will reap the benefits. I am so grateful for Victoria's transparency and love that are felt in every chapter, paragraph, and line.

Fellow mother, I stand arms locked with you as you read this book. May it be the encouragement you need in due season. May the God who governs angel armies equip you to fight well, dear mama, as you put on your armor.

From one Warrior Mother to another,
Quantrilla Ard, PhD, author, speaker, and grief coach

Battlefield Earth

THE DAY HAS COME . . .

Dressed in your armor, boots tied, helmet secured, you've realized the enemy has broken into the camp. The enemy is in your territory, and the battle ahead will be intense. Your boots are covered in mud. Your uniform is disheveled from the chaos, and your mind is racing: *What do I do now?* The intense sounds of gunshots rattle your bones. However, even louder than the sound of war is the *thump, thump, thump, thump* of your heart. The scene is more intense than any battle you could have ever imagined. Yet you continue to charge forward. You are determined to win this battle! Straggling behind you are your soldiers. Soldiers you've been placed in charge of.

Your troops are watching you as you fight the enemy fearlessly. You charge ahead, with your soldiers following closely and waiting your next command. You feel confident they will make it out of this battle. After all, they know the stories of past wars. You've taught them from your life as a soldier. They've been through various training for these moments. You think, *My squad should be ready for anything.*

Yet no sooner than this thought crosses your mind do things take a turn for the worse. You whirl to see your soldiers being bombarded with the shots of the enemy.

First your youngest soldier is hit. Although you tried to keep him sheltered the most, he wasn't mature enough for battle. His lack of knowledge of the outside world and the battles he'd face made him an easy target.

Then another falls. This one was known for being defiant. She'd failed to listen in basic training and is always certain she knows what's best. You're hurt by her pain but not surprised by her defeat.

Eager to please you, another soldier runs in front of you, only to be trapped by the enemy.

Then there's the energetic soldier. Overly excited, she makes a careless mistake that costs her life.

Then your best soldier takes a hit. Little did you know, this one has been struggling with confidence. As soon as he heard the enemy, he became too timid to fight.

One by one you've lost your soldiers to the enemy. You recognize that there is no way to save them now. Your grief, regrets, and shame of mismanaging the troops renders you ineffective to revive them. In your mind you are unfit for duty and your soldiers are prisoners of war. You fall to the ground, too shaken to move.

But before you allow yourself to be completely overtaken, you make one agonizing final plea for help. "Lord, please save my children!"

You see, these soldiers are no ordinary group, and this battle is for their very souls. These soldiers are the ones you birthed in your womb or chose through adoption. The ones who look or act like you and who you have spent your blood, sweat, and tears on. These are your babies, the ones you've been entrusted with. In your defeated state, you recognize that you had been trying to fight the war in your own strength. At times you even relied on others' strength to carry you through. Though your effort was valiant and heartfelt, it was useless without God to fight the battle on your behalf. You had been trying to be a mother and warrior on your own.

And in this moment, you hear a still, small voice inside you say, "Get up—it's time for war!" The voice reminds you that you've never been the giving-up type.

You are a warrior.

You are the mother of soldiers who need you.

You are the carrier of the love and hope needed to bring life back to your fallen troops.

Warrior Mother, it's time to head into the battlefield with your troops. In this battlefield of earth, the Enemy is pulling out all the stops to overtake your home, your children, and your very peace. I give you a warning. This is not your average parenting book. I believe the Lord is calling us to rise up and do more than just correct bad behavior. He is calling us to fight in prayer, with fasting, and with great intention.

This fight starts with self-examination and working with grit to clean up any life areas that have become a hindrance. God will move mightily in our parenting, which will impact generations to come. This choice to rise up and be warriors for Christ is one that will change the course of your life as well as your children's lives. I believe the Lord is raising up a generation of mothers who will stand for truth and fight in prayer along with action. The devil will not have the final say in our homes ever again.

Warrior Mother, enough is enough. It's time for war!

Signed courageously,
Victoria Riollano

Warrior (noun):
a person who is brave, resilient,
and actively engaged in warfare

Chapter One

UNLEASH THE WARRIOR

The Lord gives the command; the women who proclaim
good news are a great army.
PSALM 68:11 NASB

MOTHERHOOD IS NOT FOR THE faint of heart.

Time and time again, the Bible offers us stories of mothers who were willing to do the unthinkable to protect their children. These mothers were warriors in their own right. We see great heroines who took risks, thought strategically, and prayed relentlessly for the hopes of giving their children the life God had called them to.

Hagar escaped to the desert to protect Ishmael.

Jochebed placed Moses in a basket and set it in a river in hopes of saving his life.

Zipporah circumcised her child in an instant to save her family.

After years of being barren, Hannah gave her only child to the priest.

Mary lived a life on the run throughout her pregnancy and the beginning of the life of Jesus.

These stories alone remind us that the battle we face as mothers is not a new one. These women of strength, courage, poise, love, and tenacity refused to allow the Enemy to lay siege to their children. They serve as examples that whether we like it or not, the weight of motherhood is a heavy one that requires much heart.

Here is the reality of what we are up against. We have an adversary who has been in existence long before us. His tactics are not meant to just irritate you but to destroy you and your family. The Enemy's version of warfare is guerilla, with small, unexpected attacks to your finances or relationships at any given moment. Perhaps he attacks you with psychological warfare by planting thoughts that make you feel inferior. He may use biological warfare to attack your child with sickness at every turn.

As the Word of God says, the Enemy comes "only to steal and kill and destroy" (John 10:10). It is his very nature to cause destruction, and we would be foolish to believe we aren't prime targets. Let's be clear—there are three forces fighting against you at all times. The first force is your flesh, which is your innate sin nature that leads you to lie, cheat, be jealous, be quick to anger, and more. You can only outrun these tendencies by living by the Spirit and aligning yourself with God's Word. The second force is the influences of this world. This would include the power of media, demonic aspects of the culture around you (like if you grow up in a family that glorifies witchcraft), things you were taught in school, and people who affect your life in negative ways. And lastly, you have Satan and his demonic forces. This is why the Bible says, "For our struggle is not against flesh and blood, but against the rulers, against the authorities, against the powers of this dark world and against the spiritual forces of evil in the heavenly realms" (Ephesians 6:12).

Whether we like it or not, the moment we accepted Jesus into our lives and made a choice to raise children who love the Lord, we put ourselves right in the line of fire.

When it comes to Satan and his minions, this enemy force does no good. The devil has no positive thoughts toward you. He has never told you the truth, and he never will. He twists Scripture, causes havoc, and rejoices in your despair. Whether we like it or not, the moment we accepted Jesus into our lives and so made a choice to raise children who love the Lord, we put ourselves right in the line of fire.

For some this may be frightening. Yet when we recognize that the Lord is on our side and He *always* wins, we can face the Enemy fully equipped to hold our ground against every attack. A key part of war is being aware that although there are weapons created against us, we don't have to be overcome by them. In fact, we can gladly declare Isaiah 54:7 that no weapon formed against us shall prosper! "The art of war teaches us to rely not on the likelihood of the enemy's not coming, but on our own readiness to receive him; not on the chance of his not attacking, but rather on the fact that we have made our position unassailable."[1]

Warrior Mother, This Is Where We Come In

It is our job to act as the lionesses who protect their cubs from danger no matter the cost. We are their first line of defense against the Enemy. Yet in our own strength, we would find ourselves tired and defeated. The truth is, our role goes beyond protecting our children from the Enemy. We must also train them up to know how to spot the Enemy from afar and overcome his tactics. Our children are looking to us to be the spiritual and emotional backbone they need until they become adults and beyond. They are looking to us to be a place of security and peace. They are looking to us to prepare them for the battles ahead.

We often hear statistics associated with the absence of a father in the home. Many of us can quote what we've been taught about the importance of fathers helping their children to develop a sense of self-worth. Yet much less attention is given to the importance of the mother. The well-known Negro spiritual "Sometimes I Feel Like a Motherless Child" depicts this well. In the song, you can feel the anguish of the artist as she cries for the love of her mother. Being motherless is something I wouldn't wish on my worst enemy.

Research shows that the lack of a mother figure has been associated with lower self-worth, depression, and difficulties maintaining adult relationships.[2] The pain of missing such an important figure in your life is tangible and one that's not easily repaired. As a mother you must recognize that you are a vital piece of your child's foundation. Whether you are the biological mother, grandmother, spiritual mother, or foster mother, the Lord has given you a high level of authority in the lives of the children He's given you.

Just like a military squad leader, the troops in your home are looking to you for the essentials of how to move through every battle in life victoriously. For many mothers, when they consider this heavy weight of responsibility, they are instantly overwhelmed. Many are left wondering, *Am I enough?*

You may not feel like much of a warrior . . . *yet*. In fact, you may relate to the mother in the battlefield scene. You may relate to feeling like all is lost and like you can't possibly lead your troops. Your past difficult seasons in parenting may have left you feeling like no matter how hard you try, you won't measure up. You may feel like you lack the resources, training, time, or emotional support to get the job done. If you have more than one child, a child who struggles with his or her behavior, or a child who has a disability or sickness, your insecurities may be magnified. In my own life, I can say there have been moments when I thought, *I can't do this!*

Warrior Mother, the Lord wants you to know that you are enough. Before the beginning of the earth, the Lord chose you. He knew that you were the exact match for your specific child. In fact, it was no accident that He chose you to mother at this exact moment, in your exact country, in this exact moment in history. Yes, the Lord chose you to parent in a world of social media, political tensions, and influences that contradict the Word of God at every turn. Yet despite the circumstances, your past, your shortcomings, your insecurities, and your worries, God chose you. With great intentionality, He knew you would be the one to instill the needed values for your child to face the world.

You can read a thousand parenting books, go to conferences every weekend, and join mothers' groups galore, but until you accept that you are enough, it will all be worthless. This recognition does not come overnight. It will take intentional seeking of the Lord and resting in His truth over your life. (We will tackle this in a later chapter.) Today I'm asking you to make a declaration. For some, you may not believe this phrase quite yet. I challenge you to "faith it till you make it" if needed. By the end of the book, I have no doubt things will change. Say this with me: "Thank You, Lord. I am enough for my family."

Can we take a moment to just breathe in this phrase? You may need to say it repeatedly as you dive into this book. Do it! I believe every time you say this phrase, you will be empowered to keep going. God has a purpose for your children, and you are made of just the right stuff to help them accomplish it. How then do we go from mother to warrior? How do we go from barely making it through sleepless nights to being of great strength and courage? How do we become mothers empowered by the Holy Spirit against every attack of the Enemy?

My goal is for you to feel empowered to do all of the above. But before we dive in, I want to take a moment to acknowledge that I happen to be a mother of seven. I happen to have a master's degree in child and adolescent psychology. I happen to be a licensed minister and have been in ministry for two decades. Yet I *still* find myself feeling flustered with day-to-day parenting issues like bedtimes, chores, bullying, or balancing career and family. I still must cry out to the Lord and ask Him for help, a lot.

Here's the truth—I entered motherhood bright-eyed and bushy-tailed. At the age of twenty-two, I had worked in childcare for six years and was the lead teacher in an infant room at a prestigious Montessori-styled school. So I went into my first pregnancy an "expert" in developmental milestones and how to help children flourish socially and emotionally. In many ways, I thought having a baby would be the easiest thing I would ever do.

The hospital ride home from having my first child brought me back to reality. In the back seat of the car, none of the education, experience, or fantasies mattered. My mind was flooded with the weight of responsibility of taking care of this six-pound, seven-ounce human. Every doctor's appointment, how she viewed the world, what she participated in would rest in my hands. This was on top of making sure I kept this child alive! Needless to say, within five minutes of sitting beside this little one in the back seat, I let out the ugliest cry I have ever cried to date. I realized quickly that in my own strength, I could never parent my daughter. In that moment, I felt so helpless and completely in over my head. I would be lying if I said this was the only time I've felt this kind of agony of not knowing how to be the best mom.

Each year, the Lord reminded me of what I shared with you earlier— I am enough. He would guide me through every step of parenting. If only I was willing to listen and submit to Him, I would experience victory in every battle. Seven kids in, God has yet to disappoint! I am a firm believer that if He can deliver me from nights of tears, depression, and incessant worry over my children, He can do it for anyone.

I am convinced that we've been handed the responsibility of mothering not to break us but for God's glory to show through us. The battles we face are not and will not ever be too big for our God! Whether you are dealing with terrible twos, a child with a serious illness, or a teenager who has walked away from God, He can meet you and your child right where you are. He can fight on your behalf and teach you how to rise up and be the warrior you've been called to be for your children!

In order to move forward into what is required for moms to win in the spiritual and natural battles of life, we must first acknowledge three realities of war. These three aspects will be the foundation of the book and will empower you to be the champion needed for your child.

A Warrior Is Actively Involved in Warfare

A warrior would never stumble into a fight. In fact, a warrior would approach each battle with insight, strategy, wisdom, counsel, and a keen awareness of the enemy's tactics. We see this clearly in the story of David and Goliath. Although many may focus on the ending victory, few remember what David said to Saul *before* his battle with the giant Goliath.

> Your servant has been keeping his father's sheep. When a lion or a bear came and carried off a sheep from the flock, I went after it, struck it and rescued the sheep from its mouth. When it turned on me, I seized it by its hair, struck it and killed it. Your servant has killed both the lion and the bear; this uncircumcised Philistine will be like one of them, because he has defied the armies of the living God. The LORD who rescued me from the paw of the lion and the paw of the bear will rescue me from the hand of this Philistine. (1 Samuel 17:34–37)

In other words, David was active in warfare years before he ever met Goliath. He was skilled in the everyday fights that came along with his role as a shepherd. This gave him the gumption to take on what seemed to be an impossible task as he faced Goliath. Before he ever heard of the battle, he was fully aware that he had what it took to win—God on his side, and preparation!

I love what David prayed in Psalm 144:1 (NASB): "Blessed be the LORD, my rock, who trains my hands for war and my fingers for battle." If we want to stand up for our children against the Enemy, we need the Lord to teach us how to fight. In fact, you will never find a soldier who didn't complete some form of training. From boot camp to proper ways to use a weapon, to how to fight combatively, a soldier trains for war on purpose. I know this well, as I reside just moments from Marine Corps Base Quantico. At any given minute, I can hear the thundering booms of explosive demolitions and rapid-fire gun drills—loud enough to make our home rattle. Although this was once unsettling, it's clear that the marines are always training and preparing for the day when a war may be at hand.

So when it comes to motherhood, reading this book is simply not enough. Listening to parenting podcasts or reading blogs on motherhood won't do! Instead, immersing yourself in the Word of God, praying intently, and using the methods God teaches you will be key aspects of your hands being "trained for war."

There Are Many Strategies to War

Depending on the era and the specific country, you will find different methods of war. Aerial warfare, trench warfare, chemical warfare, and biological warfare are just some ways wars have been fought. Today warfare goes beyond the traditional methods and seeks to attack information and systems. The invention of the internet has brought in a new wave of attacks called cyberwarfare, where technology and political systems can be hacked to cause havoc.

Warfare comes in many packages and is not intended to be pretty or to cause minimal damage. War is active, strategic, and purposeful. Even guerilla warfare, a type used by small groups of untrained civilians, has an element of banding together to conduct ambushes and spark fires among enemy forces. In other words, when it comes to war, fighting fair is not the goal—winning is.

Just as countries fight wars with crafty strategies to bring the most damage, we have an adversary who seeks to do the same. However, we can rise up, knowing that God also has a plan. When it comes to the spiritual battles we face, we can win. God has shown us in His Word that we are not helpless victims. We are victorious women armed for battle, if we choose to pick up our weaponry. But we don't fight with natural weapons. We fight differently! From prayer to fasting, to standing in faith, to declaring the Word of God, we employ tactics at every turn. My job throughout this book is to enlighten you about the many approaches you can use to see victory in your parenting.

War Will Cost You Something

There is no way around the cost of war. In the United States alone, it is estimated that the cost of post-9/11 counterterrorism actions is over $6 trillion.[3] This doesn't factor in the more than eight hundred thousand lives lost in the mission nor the social, political, or economic impact. In every war, resources are needed, and people are required on the front lines and behind the scenes. Going into war, countries are aware that someone must be willing to pay for the personnel, weaponry, and damage caused.

Even now, as you're reading this, the Lord may be highlighting an area of your life that you must be willing to forfeit to gain the victory. Much like countries that enter into war, we must know there will be necessary sacrifices. Embrace this fact of life. Your role is to protect the troops in your care no matter the cost. I want to challenge you with this question: What is God calling you to release? It could be the habit that causes your child to not respect you as she should. The Lord could be speaking to you about living arrangements that may be dishonoring Him. It may even be necessary to remove some friendships and relationships that are inflicting pain on those in your care. In this battle, if we expect business as usual, with a dash of prayer, we will be disappointed. Instead, we need to actively seek His face for what must be kept and what must be laid down. Letting go of what God is trying to remove is not defeat—it's victory.

As we continue through the next few chapters, my prayer is that you are empowered to pray in a new way and to see your children for who they really are in the eyes of the Lord. Remember, you don't need a degree in child development, you aren't required to memorize the Bible from front to back, and you do not need a lifetime of experience to see victory in your parenting. I am convinced you will find everything you need, and all the strength required, through the Word of God. No matter how your circumstances look right now, this is the moment to see things shift in a radical way for yourself and your children. Let us fight in prayer and action like their lives depend on it. Together, as we rise up and proclaim God's truth over our families, we can be a great army.

You are a warrior!

————————— VICTORY VERSE —————————

"No weapon forged against you will prevail, and you will refute every tongue that accuses you. This is the heritage of the servants of the LORD, and this is their vindication from me," declares the LORD. (Isaiah 54:17)

—————————————— REFLECTIONS ——————————————

1. In what areas of parenting do you feel insufficient (finances, emotional support, biblical knowledge)?
2. Which aspect of war challenges you the most?
3. Is the Lord calling you to give something up to fight for your child(ren)?

—————————————— POWER PRAYER ——————————————

Lord, I thank You for _____. I ask that You speak Your truth over my life and _____'s life. Remind me that You are on my side. Teach me to trust You in my parenting journey. I need Your help to learn how to war for my children. Lord, will You teach my hands to war and my fingers to battle? If there are things within me that are keeping me from being effective in my parenting, I ask that You highlight those areas in my life and give me the strength to overcome. In Jesus's name. Amen.

Chapter Two

KNOW YOUR PLACE

Conversion is a complete surrender to Jesus. It's a
willingness to do what He wants you to do.
BILLY SUNDAY

KNOW YOUR PLACE.

This phrase is typically used to demean or belittle. Knowing one's place entails staying in line and living under the authority of another person. In most cases, if you are being told to "know your place," it's not a good thing.

Anyone who's attended a military boot camp will attest that they realized they were not in charge shortly after saying their oath to service. Occasionally I'll ask my husband about his boot camp experience. Without a doubt he'll have a funny story about being made to eat his meals while staring directly into the eyes of another recruit or being called "Grandpa" because he was the oldest recruit in his company. Yet out of all the boot camp moments, he shares the words of his company commanders the most: "Do what you're told, how you're told, when you're told." This was not just the motto—it was the expectation. By enlisting in the military, he needed to be aware that what he thought was the best and what he believed he should be doing at any given moment was not necessarily correct. His company commanders knew exactly what was needed to prepare him to go from an untrained recruit to being ready for the missions ahead. It was essential that he submitted his will and momentary desires to the company command-ers. If he didn't, he would fail to learn the military basics, protocol, and expectations. He had to recognize his place as a newly enlisted military member and respect the authority of those in his chain of command.

As you're reading, I want to pause and respectfully challenge your place in terms of motherhood.

Here's the truth—from the moment we learn we're going to be moth-ers, we take full ownership of our children. We realize quickly that moth-erhood is a full-time career with a job description that includes nurse, chef, counselor, coach, assistant, chauffeur, and more. In many ways we empty ourselves out for these little ones with no strings attached. In fact, we love it. No matter how tired we may be, there is a thrill that comes along with being such a vital piece of someone else's life. Even on our most difficult days, being a mother gives us something to live for wholeheartedly. As a mother, I can honestly say that no matter how frustrated I might be with my child who loves to scream through the house, the other who refuses to sleep in her own bed, or the preteen who hates cleaning with a passion, one hug from them dispels all irritation. Our children easily become the objects of our affection, and at some moments it feels like our lives revolve around helping them succeed.

In walks the bad news: our children do not belong to us.

Before you throw your book down, I want to preface this by say-ing your role in your child's life can never be diminished or taken for granted. You are the one who carried your child in the womb or who purposefully chose to take in your child. There is no greater love on earth than a mother's for her child. Yet all in all, as much as we would love to believe that our children are our personal projects to groom to our liking, they are not.

Your child unequivocally and wholeheartedly belongs to the Lord. In His great wisdom and love,

He chose to bless you with a person you could pour into.
He chose to make you the example of His heart toward each
   child in your care.

He chose you to give instruction.

He chose you to carry wisdom that would sustain your child throughout life.

He chose you to see the best in your child when no one else does.

He chose you to pray and intercede on your child's behalf.

He chose you to instill values and principles that honor Him.

Yet, though He chose you for this, He never completely relinquished His rights to you. God still has and always will have the deepest investment in your child. In fact, we see that His eyes have been watching over our children from the womb (Jeremiah 1:5). Each tiny person was created with a plan, talents, and purpose to be fulfilled.

Before you ever laid eyes on your child, the Lord thought about her in great detail and delighted over her life. He knew your son's intimate thoughts before you could even understand his first word. God knew the sound of your daughter's cry before she took her first breath. He knew who your child would grow up to marry before you knew whether you would have a girl or a boy.

This is where we insert a praise break. What great love is this! Our God, the Creator, the King of Kings, knew your children intricately *before* they were even born.

Not only does He know them so well that even the hairs on their heads are numbered, but He also has a plan for them. God has a specific, personal, well-thought-out plan. He tells us, "'For I know the plans I have for you,' declares the LORD, 'plans to prosper you and not to harm you, plans to give you hope and a future'" (Jeremiah 29:11).

You are a part of this plan. However, you are not the creator of the plan. Neither are you solely responsible for seeing this plan come to fruition. Your role is to lay the foundation for your children to walk into God's design for their lives. From being a mother who operates in wisdom to nurturing your children with grace and truth, you've been granted the responsibility to help them reach the maturity and character for their journeys ahead. Yet you are tasked to parent in a way where your will is fully submitted to God's plan. For this reason, I say it again—we must know our place.

Are you at a place where you can "do what you're told, how you're told, when you're told," as the Lord leads you to? Have you reached a point of total submission and surrender in your parenting? This is not said to diminish your role as a mother but to encourage you to recognize that you are not on this journey alone. When we surrender to the Lord in our parenting, we seek Him regularly for what's best. We talk to Him about His children and how He wants them to be raised. And when He speaks, we respond. I have to be honest—there were many times I thought I was trusting God for my parenting only to learn I was the one in charge. There have even been times I have taken matters into my own hands by not praying about big decisions and by allowing my emotions or even the pressures of the world to dictate my parenting. Sadly, when things went wrong, I blamed the Lord rather than my choice not to follow His direction. Fortunately, I didn't stay in this place. And after a series of events with my daughter, the way I see God's role in my parenting has changed forever.

We Lead the Troops, but God Is the Commander

The Lord is alongside you every step of the way. He is invested more than you can even imagine in seeing your children grow into their fullest potential. Years ago I came to terms with this firsthand when my daughter Trinity had unexplained seizures. It was a busy Saturday morning with many errands on our to-do list. At this point, we only had three children. Trinity was four at the time and probably the most well-mannered and sweetly spirited child I had ever interacted with. Yet this morning she was extraordinarily fussy and seemed to need a bathroom break every twenty minutes. Even after our second time pulling over, she still had accidents in the local dollar store twice. Needless to say, I was frustrated that my day wasn't going perfectly and annoyed that my child who was fully potty trained was having accidents all over town. We drove home, and I went straight to my room with the youngest baby, while my husband prepared the children for nap time. Typically I would pray over my children before they slept. However, that day, in my anger and frustration, I shut myself off from everyone.

Within thirty minutes my husband screamed my name. I instantly knew something was wrong with Trinity. As I rushed into her room, I saw the most horrific sight. She was having a grand mal seizure—unresponsive, eyes rolling back, and convulsing from head to toe. I couldn't believe it. In my mind, I believed she would never be the same. Would she dance like a ballerina or sing again? Would she run or graduate high school? Why did I spend so much time being angry at her accidents earlier versus inquiring what could be wrong? I was overwhelmed with guilt.

After Trinity spent four days in the hospital, doctors could not determine what had caused the seizure and sent us home with the assumption it would never happen again. Trinity appeared to return to her normal self. However, after six months she had another seizure. This one was more severe than the last. A decision was made by the doctors to put her on medication. Without the medication, she could have more seizures in her sleep, with irreversible and deadly consequences.

After the second seizure, I was on a mission to ensure this never happened again. I spent many nights relentlessly watching over the baby monitor. I ordered monitors for under her mattress and special seizure pillows from Switzerland. I researched endlessly everything I could do in my power not to allow another episode. In my own words, "My daughter will not die on my watch." This lasted a few years, and eventually a deep depression overtook me.

Unfortunately, I was not alone. An estimated 7.5 million parents in the United States struggle with depression. This depression affects the parent's ability to nurture, provide material needs for, and sustain a healthy relationship with their child, along with many other challenges that affect the overall well-being of the child and the family.[1] I experienced these things during this season. The sleepless nights, needing to keep Trinity in arm's reach at all times, paying less attention to the others in my family who needed me, and the paralyzing fear were weighing heavily on my heart. One day in a moment of despair, I cried out to God. He spoke to my heart.

"Will you trust me with my daughter? Do you know that I love her more than you ever can? Do you believe I can heal her? Do you know none of this caught me by surprise? Will you allow me to take this burden from you?"

This realization that I served a God who loved my child more than I ever could was mind-blowing. Here's the thing—I knew this in Bible-knowledge terms, yet I had never accepted that God took magnificent pleasure in watching over my daughter and bringing the healing she needed. I stand here today to say releasing that burden and letting God have His rightful place as her Father was the most freeing experience. The Lord showed me that I no longer needed to parent her in fear. No matter what the outcome would be, I could trust Him completely. Trinity has now been seizure-free for a decade. I am thankful to say that after ten years of medication and years of prayer, she is no longer considered epileptic and has no adverse symptoms from her seizures. She is completely healed!

I want to pause and speak to those who don't have the same testimony as my own. Maybe you are still waiting for God to move miraculously for your child, or perhaps your child has already gone to be with the Lord. Truthfully, I know that not everyone's story will end with the miraculous healing we hope for. In these moments, I ask the Lord to show me how He did move and how He did show His love in ways that maybe went unnoticed. Perhaps for you it was how He brought you through the tragedy or the way He led you to encourage those facing similar situations. Maybe it was through a doctor who showed you the love of God and supported you in your lowest moments. We can find strength in knowing that although we may not have received the outcome we wanted, God was with us every step of the way. He is not dismissive or unaware of our circumstances. My prayer is that no matter how difficult the pain of waiting to see how God reveals Himself in your child's story, you never forget He is still in control and somehow will use even the lowest moments for His glory. And as He reminded me, He has an everlasting love for your child. May you remain firm that God is with you every step of the way and guiding you through even the toughest valleys.

No matter how your parenting has gone thus far, I implore you to allow the Lord to be the leader of your parenting journey. The truth is that surrendering our parenting to God will be the best choice we can ever make. When we recognize our role in the parenting paradigm, we can release the pressure of needing to have all the answers and solve every issue in our own limited strength. It's from this place that we can begin to fully rely on the Lord for instruction. Instead of approaching God begging for help, we know He is with us in the trenches. Just like with my daughter, He was fully engaged in every step and ready to allow every moment to be used for His glory. When I surrendered my desperate need to be in control, I found true peace and victory.

Hannah's Story

Recognizing that our children belong fully to God is not a new concept. In 1 Samuel we see Hannah made a conscious choice that she and her future children belonged to God. Hannah made a vow, even before she became pregnant, to dedicate her son to the Lord. "And she made a vow, saying, 'LORD Almighty, if you will only look on your servant's misery and remember me, and not forget your servant but give her a son, then I will give him to the LORD for all the days of his life, and no razor will ever be used on his head'" (1 Samuel 1:11).

Hannah transitioned from years of barrenness to giving birth to a son, Samuel. Once she'd finished weaning Samuel, she took him to the house of the Lord (just as she had promised God) and gave him away. She literally gave away the baby she had begged God for. Can you imagine? Many would have been kicking and screaming during the entire process, but Hannah's immediate response after she gave away her son was this prayer: "My heart rejoices in the LORD" (1 Samuel 2:1).

Hannah was joyful after dedicating her child to God. She knew deep down that Samuel would benefit greatly from this choice. Amazingly, Samuel would grow up to be one of the greatest prophets of the Old Testament. God, in His goodness, didn't just stop there with Hannah. He rewarded her willingness to relinquish control of Samuel by giving her many more sons and daughters. Though we aren't physically dropping off our children at the local church to be raised by the pastor, there is much we can learn from Hannah. Hannah knew her place.

When it comes to your own children, are you aware of your role as a mother? Do you believe you are your child's Holy Spirit? Do you seldom seek their Creator for answers to everyday issues? Are you hesitant to relinquish control to God? Do you feel like God may not be paying enough attention to your child's needs? Do you *really* trust that He is a good God and faithful to protect them? Do you consult with Him before making major life decisions concerning His children? The answers, though stinging, can be the difference between parenting in defeat versus parenting victoriously.

We must love our children enough to allow God to take the lead, much like we see in Hannah's story. She was willing to fully submit her parenting to the Lord. This doesn't mean we are quiet or reserved in our parenting. This means we actively seek the face of God for every move regarding our children. Whether we're considering team sports, homeschooling, or sleepovers, some decisions may seem simple but can have a lasting impact on their lives. What if we ask the Lord for guidance every step of the way? Though it may feel like this is an act of becoming powerless, it is quite the opposite.

Align Yourself with Heaven

Although we often think of the mama bear as the symbol of strength and protection for children, this is nothing compared to a mother who is led by the Holy Spirit in all her ways. It's not enough to simply want

God to do remarkable things for our children—we need to take the extra step and allow our hearts to be surrendered to His will for them.

I leave you with one more example.

Imagine you had a personal relationship with the late Steve Jobs, cofounder and CEO of Apple. Suppose Mr. Jobs created a brand-new cell phone model and handed it to you to take care of. Though you would get to know the features of the phone, you wouldn't be the creator. You would never have full ownership of the product. You would simply be the person responsible for the phone for the time being. In some ways, this would be freeing because you would know that Mr. Jobs would be a source of information at any moment. You would trust that Mr. Jobs would have the perfect answer if any issues arose. Furthermore, you would have no doubt that he was 100 percent aware of the inner workings of the phone and his plan for its usage. Simply by knowing this, your personal relationship with him and awareness of his role would give you a great amount of confidence.

Just like the example implies, we must be aware of who ultimately has the answers. When we recognize that we have a loving Father who values His creations, we can take a breath of relief, knowing that He is leading the charge. Much like the Steve Job's example, God is fully aware of all the inner workings of your individual child and the plans He has for your family. Our job is to make a choice to relinquish control of it all and submit our plans for our children to His authority. Submitting your will to God will be the most impactful choice you will ever make. There is beauty in your surrender.

Knowing His Voice

Here's what I've learned. We must stay in a position of knowing what God is speaking. So I challenge you today with this: How can we combat negative thoughts with God's Word if we don't know it for ourselves? How can we lead children into victory when we don't even know the words of the ultimate commander, God Himself? Remember, the brain can adapt to our thoughts. We must intentionally retrain our minds to default to God's Word over our lives and our children's lives. Yet the only way we can do so is if we spend time reading the Bible, become intentional about prayer, and write what He is speaking.

I encourage you to keep a journal and record what God has spoken over your life. You can also use sticky notes to write out promises of God and put them in strategic places around your home. One way to face the battles ahead in stride will be to build your confidence in His Word. His words are always true and are always accomplished—your job is to believe them. "God is not human, that he should lie, not a human being, that he should change his mind. Does he speak and then not act? Does he promise and not fulfill?" (Numbers 23:19).

In order to follow God's lead for your child, you must be willing to focus on your own relationship with God.

Surrender doesn't come without great intention and a full reliance on the Lord. In order to follow God's lead for your child, you must be willing to focus on your own relationship with God. By reading His Word, making the choice to seek Him in prayer and devotion, you will learn His voice and know what to do and how to do it. As Jesus said, "My sheep listen to my voice; I know them, and they follow me" (John 10:27). It will be impossible to know what God wants for your child if you aren't even aware of His heart and plans for you. We make a grave mistake as mothers when we want our children to have a deep relationship with God but don't have one ourselves. Let us be purposeful about setting aside intentional time to know God's heart, His character, and His voice. If we refuse to do so, we will never quite walk in the full surrender required to parent victoriously.

Think on the words spoken by my husband's company commander years ago: "Do what you're told, how you're told, when you're told."

When it comes to our Christian parenting journey, we must know that God is our commander in chief and ultimate authority. He is in charge and charting the paths. Our job is to carry out the mission at hand—raise children who live out their God-given destiny. There is so much freedom in allowing God to take the lead in your parenting journey. Pray and listen to the Lord every step of the way and watch Him lead you into great victory. Simply said, do what God says, how He says it, when He says it.

VICTORY VERSES

For you created my inmost being;
    you knit me together in my mother's womb.
I praise you because I am fearfully and wonderfully made;
    your works are wonderful,
    I know that full well.
My frame was not hidden from you
    when I was made in the secret place,
    when I was woven together in the depths of the earth.
Your eyes saw my unformed body;
    all the days ordained for me were written in your book
    before one of them came to be.
How precious to me are your thoughts, God!
    How vast is the sum of them!
Were I to count them,
    they would outnumber the grains of sand—
    when I awake, I am still with you. (Psalm 139:13–18)

REFLECTIONS

1. Do you wholeheartedly trust the Lord with your child? Are there any areas in which you have hesitation?
2. Have there been times where you doubted whether God had your child's best interest in mind?
3. How would your life look if you fully relied on the Lord for plans concerning your child?

─────────────── POWER PRAYER ───────────────

God, I thank You for allowing me to mother _____. I don't take this opportunity for granted. Lord, I give my baby over to You. Though it may be scary to relinquish control, I trust You. I trust Your heart for my child. I trust that You will protect _____ when I cannot. I trust that You will comfort _____ when I don't have the words to say. I believe that You will lead my child to a deep relationship with You day by day. Teach me to love and nurture in the way that _____ needs. Help me to see You as the Creator and Father who loves my child with an undying love. Forgive me for the times I didn't seek You for instruction. I ask that Your peace rest over me. I thank You for this beautiful surrender. For I know that if You are by _____'s side, I have nothing to worry about. In Jesus's name. Amen.

Chapter Three

WAR PLAN

Strategy without tactics is the slowest route to victory.
Tactics without strategy is the noise before defeat.
SUN TZU, *THE ART OF WAR*

THE FAMOUS QUOTE ABOVE SHOULD speak volumes to us. You and I must have a plan. It's that simple.

We are not the first or last mothers on earth who've realized that parenting requires a willingness to make a plan and stick to it. Let's consider the story of Jochebed in Exodus 1:8–22. But before we talk about how God used this mother's plan in his own plan for history, let's explore the backstory. At this juncture in history, the Israelites had been slaves in Egypt for hundreds of years. Although the king of Egypt may have enjoyed using slaves to handle the needs of Israel, he realized they were growing in number. He feared there would be a day when the Hebrew slaves would be uncontainable, even partnering with a foreign army to overtake the Egyptians. Nervous that the Egyptian kingdom could lose control, he devised a plan to create more grueling labor. Yet instead of shrinking back, the Israelites multiplied more than ever. When creating a harsher work environment did not work, the king decided that the only way to truly attack them was by cutting off their generations. "The king of Egypt said to the Hebrew midwives, whose names were Shiphrah and Puah, 'When you are helping the Hebrew women during childbirth on the delivery stool, if you see that the baby is a boy, kill him; but if it is a girl, let her live'" (Exodus 1:15–17).

Yet the pair of brave midwives disobeyed and let every child live. Although this gained them favor with the Lord, it infuriated the king. Running out of ideas, he ordered everyone to throw newborn male children into the river. We can only imagine how this caused strife and turmoil within the Israelite camp as they were forced to follow the king's decree. Expecting mothers would now spend the last few moments of their pregnancies in terror. For if the children they were carrying were boys, they would be doomed only moments after birth. With an intimidated king wreaking havoc, midwives refusing to do the pharaoh's dirty work, neighbors turning on neighbors, and young boys being slaughtered by the masses, one mother decided to make a daring choice. "Now a man of the tribe of Levi married a Levite woman, and she became pregnant and gave birth to a son. When she saw that he was a fine child, she hid him for three months. But when she could hide him no longer, she got a papyrus basket for him and coated it with tar and pitch. Then she placed the child in it and put it among the reeds along the bank of the Nile" (Exodus 2:1–3).

Jochebed made a choice to save her son. In a time of much calamity and fear, Jochebed hid her child away until the right moment, gathered the materials, created a waterproof basket, and placed it in a strategic spot. In this cleverly crafted plan, she trusted that the Lord would protect him. In true fashion, the Lord blessed Jochebed's effort and allowed the pharaoh's daughter to stumble upon the basket. This child would be named Moses. The very one who would guide the Israelites out of slavery through the Red Sea and become their leader as they journeyed to the land promised to them generations before. This would be the same Moses who would encounter God's presence and deliver His law—the Ten Commandments—to the people. Little did Jochebed know, her choice didn't just save an infant. It changed a nation for generations to come.

Jochebed had a plan. She didn't just hope that God would save her child. Neither did she just pray her way through a devastating situation. She was willing to do what needed to be done. Risking being caught and facing serious consequences, she must have known there was something special about Moses and she needed to protect him by any means necessary. Rather than stick with the status quo and hand her child over to what the culture around her demanded, she thought strategically. From knowing exactly how to hide her child and crafting a basket that could withstand the water to contemplating a suitable time of day when he might be found, Jochebed thought out every step. She learned, like so many even to this day, the power of planning, following through, and trusting God.

The Power of Vision

Years ago when my husband and I began our church, we quickly realized that we needed to put a plan in motion. It would take a combination of people, wisdom, location, finances, and goal setting to see it all come together. One of our first meetings to gain insight was with Pastor Kevin Bordeaux of Thrive Church in Richmond, Virginia. With many successful church launches under his belt in multiple church locations, and being a trendsetter for his own denomination, he came full of wisdom. Interestingly, he was less concerned about the number of people on our launch team or even our finances. He wanted to know our plan for our personal lives.

Pastor Kevin shared the importance of creating a daily plan. He explained how his daily life was highly organized with details about where he should be at what time, who he should be talking to, and even when he should be praying. Although there were times of spontaneity, he knew that when it came to life and ministry, great things didn't just happen. His words taught us that if we wanted our church plant to succeed, we needed to pray about all the details, put things in writing, and empower those around us to run with the vision the Lord had given them.

The apostle Paul exemplified this concept in 1 Corinthians 9. As Paul shared about his ministry, desire to serve God's people, and willingness to do whatever was needed to preach the gospel, he said, "I do everything to spread the Good News and share in its blessings. Don't you realize that in a race everyone runs, but only one person gets the prize? So run to win! All athletes are disciplined in their training. They do it to win a prize that will fade away, but we do it for an eternal prize. So I run with purpose in every step. I am not just shadowboxing" (1 Corinthians 9:23–26 NLT).

Paul told the Corinthian church to "run to win." For us mothers, it's not enough just to run our course of parenting for the sake of doing so. We have to run with purpose, intention, and strategy, and at a reasonable pace. It may be that part of the reason we're so exhausted is because we are waking up each day simply trying to survive. Although we may desire our children to be saved and to resist the schemes of the Enemy, we have no plans. As Paul said, we are running aimlessly and like one "shadowboxing." With no clear end goal in mind, we can't truly lead our children. How can you lead a person to a destination that you are unaware of?

The Enemy's Plan

We have been entrusted with one of the most important jobs on earth—to train and raise children to be warriors for Christ. I must admit, it took years for me to have a sense of focus when it came to my children's spiritual health. After all, everyday tasks like keeping up with laundry, helping with their schoolwork, and managing my own spiritual and emotional health are enough to make anyone completely overwhelmed. No matter what all you have on your plate, I want to encourage you to pause and seek the Lord for a clear, well-thought-out plan for those in your care. Here's what I've learned over the past few years. If we don't create a plan for our children, the Enemy will.

In the case of the Egyptian pharaoh, he was relentless in destroying the children of Israel. First he oppressed them with hard labor, then he instructed the midwives to kill the children, and then he placed the charge on everyone under his leadership to destroy the

Hebrew families. He was willing to do whatever it took to wreak havoc and ensure that his agenda was complete. In the same way, the Enemy is still at work today to rob God's children of their joy, peace, and destiny. This is where we must stand firm and say, "Not in my house" and "Not with my child!" First Peter 5:8 says, "Be alert and of sober mind. Your enemy the devil prowls around like a roaring lion looking for someone to devour."

If we don't create a plan for our children, the Enemy will.

When we accept the fact there is a real enemy who's out to destroy our families, we are left with a choice. We can either develop a sense of pessimistic doom and pray it all works out, or we can take ownership and be willing to do what's needed to protect our children. I want to encourage you to take the next step and seek the Lord for His vision for each child in your care. The prayer is simple: "Lord, reveal Your plans for my child." Then you wait, listen, and respond.

War Plan

I wonder how Jochebed went from knowing Moses was called to greatness, to creating the specific plan we see unfold in her story, to doing something about it. We must be willing to put some action behind the plan and consider small steps we can take toward getting our children to where God has called them. Ultimately it will be their choice to move as they mature and become more independent. However, until then we can be intentional about creating opportunities for growth and success. I want to note that this plan isn't about seeing them do what their hearts desire. We must also see this plan like one preparing troops for war. So as the Enemy attempts to attack your children and their destinies, you can refer back to your guide and proclaim victory over the Enemy. Writing out a plan is how you can empower your parenting journey. There are four essentials your war plan should contain.

1. A Foundational Verse

As the Lord reveals His plan for your child, I suggest you also seek Him for a Bible verse to stand on. This can be done for each individual child, for the family as a whole, or for both. In my home, our family verse is Colossians 3:23 (NLT): "Work willingly at whatever you do, as though you were working for the Lord rather than for people." With this in mind, I am able to filter every situation and difficulty through this verse. Many times when I am dealing with my children, I hear that still, small voice reminding me of this verse: "Do it for the Lord."

For my children, the verse that resonates in my heart is found in Psalm 139:13, which tells us that God knew us even when we were in our mothers' wombs. That verse reminds me that no matter what our family faces, God knew us in our most fragile moments, and He saw purpose in us. This verse reminds me that He loves my children and cares for them and that I need to seek Him for all things concerning them. It also lets me know that if my children are so special to Him that He knew them before I ever heard them utter their first cries, He has no issue fighting on their behalf.

As you can see, your foundational verse will bring strength and remind you of God's words. Before you write any other plans, be sure to find Scriptures that speak life to your parenting journey.

2. A Mission Statement

Every successful organization has a mission statement. Ranging from a sentence to a paragraph, this statement is a concise explanation of the organization's overall purpose and values. Thus, using what God has spoken about your child, you can easily create a mission statement that can speak vision. In business, mission statements have two primary goals: to motivate the participants and to ensure that outside sources know what to expect when they interact with the company. Having a mission statement can do the same for your family. It can get your child excited about the future and serve as a reminder that the Enemy will not have control over your child's life. Your child needs to hear this from you and learn to understand what it means for his or her life.

If you have older children, I encourage you to get them involved in this step. Remember, this is not about you asserting your will over them but about partnering with them to see God's will for their lives. Again, we are using God's revealed vision as the foundation for what we write. You can also observe areas where your children thrive and their personality strengths and include this in your mission statement. I want to give you a few examples of family and individual mission statements that can help you in this part of your journey.

- The Stevens family exists to help people experience God's love through art, prayer, and community service.
- Ella was created to bring joy and restoration to the world around her.
- Christian was born with a brilliant mind and focuses well. He uses the resources around him to design projects that inspire people to have wonder. Through this, many people shall give God glory.
- Aaron is a young man who inspires through music. His passion for God's people gives him determination to see tasks through and empower others in their callings.
- The Hill family walks in wellness. They exist to help people find strength and beauty in God's creation. Through prayer, intentional seeking of the Lord, and faith, they realize they can do all things through Christ.

3. Child-Specific Goals

For this next part, take a moment to create at least six clear goals for your child. These goals can have a focus on current observed needs, character development, or long-term desires. I've seen firsthand the power of goal-setting in my children's lives. For one of my children, when he was tasked with homework, I would often find him in tears. Eventually I realized he was having a tough time with reading. Not only was he struggling, but he was also two grade levels behind. It was important that I respond to this issue before it was too late. I set three goals based on need, character formation, and long-term desire.

- I will assist my child with reading at grade level within the next twelve months.
- I will seek strategy for how to help my child walk in resilience and joy when tasks are difficult.
- My child will read and write fluently, and this will be a part of his testimony later in life.

I used these three goals as an encouragement and a platform for my interactions. Rather than grow frustrated or punish him when he messed up, I had to remember that I was trying to instill in him resilience and joy. I found fun books, used his enjoyment of building to find games that pieced words together, and rewarded him for doing well. These goals helped him get to where he was going and kept me in line. Oh yes, these goals are also about you! As you are creating them and acting on them, the Lord will simultaneously be working in your heart and challenging you with how you are stewarding His children.

4. Nonnegotiables

Last, I want you to write a list of your current nonnegotiables. These are the things that are not allowed, tolerated, or promoted in your home. Period. For some mothers I have met, this is no social media in any form until the age of sixteen. For others, it's no dating until eighteen. Perhaps you have a no-sleepovers rule or a no-closed-doors policy. Only you know the convictions God has placed in your house for your child. These won't be the same for every home, every child, or even every season. Times change, and situations require shifts in rules. However, I encourage you to really let your "no be no." In fact, I want you to pause right now and practice saying no. You can say it loud, soft, slow, or fast, but get very used to saying no.

Your nonnegotiables are not there to punish or to cause your children to have a difficult life. Your nos are to protect. Let's reconsider the story of Jochebed. It is apparent that allowing infant Moses out of her sight or taking him outside was out of the question. If she had been seen with him, it would have been a life-or-death situation. In the same way, the convictions the Lord has put in your heart are to be taken seriously. You never want to find yourself in the position where you allow yourself to be talked out of your conviction and something goes wrong. In a day and age in which children are preyed upon daily in media with images that don't glorify God, and are sex-trafficked and bullied online, you have to make a choice to say no and mean it from the depths of your soul. Again, this is so that you can see God's will enacted in their lives. I believe that if there is a time to pivot or change your mind about a scenario, the Lord Himself will reveal it to you. Although your children may not understand, you protect them because you love them. Your no today will set them up for success and victory tomorrow if you hold the line and don't grow weary. Own your no and stand firm on the expectations for your home.

Taking Ownership

I will never forget how one day years ago, creating a plan changed my life and the way I interacted with my children. On this day, I began a journey in my home. During a time when I felt like my home was in disarray and I was losing touch with my children's needs, I realized that I had to pray like never before. I decided that it was time to really take ownership of my role as a mother and do what was needed to guide them closer to God's plan for their lives. With my children's pictures hung on the wall, I turned up the worship music, went to each picture, and asked the Lord for insight for each child. With tear-filled eyes, I couldn't believe how the Lord revealed His love for them and His great plans.

As I started with my oldest daughter's picture, the Lord showed me a beautiful vision of how He loved to see her spin like a ballerina and that He had created her to make beautiful moments through art.

For my second-oldest son, the Lord showed me how He created him to build and construct in ways that would change the surface of the nation. And for my youngest child, God revealed that my son would always have a way with people and that he would have great favor in business. From that moment on, I've always held to the fact that God has a plan for their lives that is specifically designed for them. Areas where they blossomed or even struggled now would be used for the glorious unfolding of His work later. Although I was only given a glimpse of what God wants to do in their lives, it empowered me as a mother to partner with them in prayer and in action.

I want to encourage you today to lean into the message found in Habakkuk: "Then the LORD said to me, 'Write my answer plainly on tablets, so that a runner can carry the correct message to others'" (Habakkuk 2:2 NLT).

Once I made the choice to intentionally seek the Lord for His plan for His children (remember, they all belong to Him), I was able to have a clear starting point to pray into their God-given destinies. I believe that part of the reason we are so lost and overwhelmed when it comes to parenting is because we have never stopped to ask for the Lord's wisdom. I can assure you that a word from Him about your child will alter the course of your parenting journey if you allow it. "If any of you lacks wisdom, you should ask God, who gives generously to all without finding fault, and it will be given to you" (James 1:5).

As we end the chapter, I want to encourage you with how I have seen victory when it comes to enacting our family's war plan. A couple of years ago, months after hearing the Lord for my daughter Trinity's life, I noticed a behavior change. She went from chipper and engaging to cold and distant. She was frustrated about going to church and had lost her interest in things that once brought her joy, like painting and dancing. Her attitude was becoming quite snappy. Honestly, I didn't always respond well to this new version of my old-est daughter. Many told me, "It's just a tween thing. Give her space. She will grow out of it." Yet my heart knew I was losing connection with her, and something wasn't right.

I sought the Lord for what to do. I remembered my own journey as a teen and how a bad attitude spawned an unruly girl who caused much pain to her mother. Opening up my journal, I was reminded of what the Lord had revealed months prior: "He created her to make beautiful moments through art." I considered the verse He had given our family years before in Colossians 3:23: "Whatever we do, do it unto the Lord" (my paraphrase). I was on a mission not to allow her passion to die, while simultaneously remembering that I needed to parent in a way that honored the Lord. I asked the Lord for a strategy on how to reconcile our relationship and help her blossom. He reminded me of how He loved watching her spin. What seemed completely irrelevant in the moment would be a key in overcoming this battle. In my mind I asked, *What does a child dancing have to do with my preteen who has become rude, melancholy, and disrespectful?* But I trusted the Lord.

Within days I enrolled Trinity in ballet class. Over the next few weeks, I saw a change. She was full of joy after each practice, sharing about the new moves she'd learned and the friends she'd made, which would become the highlight of each week. Yet what was even more beautiful were the hours spent in the car during that season. Each visit to ballet brought more one-on-one time and intimate conversations. I watched the Lord soften Trinity's heart again, and my own. To this day, years later, her attitude has never reverted back to that season. I believe the Lord gave me the word for her to dance—not just for her enjoyment but as a first step for what He wanted to do in her life. Her joy is radiant, she excels in dance, and she even releases her own music. God's vision of her creating through art is literally unfolding before my eyes. Yet it didn't just happen—it took intentional prayer *and* action. I could have listened to those around me who encouraged me to give her space. Yet that was the opposite of what she needed, which was a connection and a mother who would love her in a way that reflected Colossians 3:23. God's word for her life and our foundational verse were more than enough to initiate a transformation.

Warrior Mother, after you write this plan, I need you to own it! Make a choice to hold on to hope even if it goes against the culture and human logic. This war plan will be like a sword in your hand and empower you to say no. By having a plan to stand on, you will be able to pivot and initiate small steps to move you toward your goal, like I did with my Trinity. You will also have a strategy to not allow anything that contradicts what God has spoken over your children. In fact, if anyone speaks a word that belittles or does not line up with God's vision, you will quickly know it's from the Enemy. Stand strong, pray like their lives depend on it, and create action steps to lead them toward victory!

─────────────── VICTORY VERSES ───────────────

Whatever you do, work at it with all your heart, as working for the Lord, not for human masters, since you know that you will receive an inheritance from the Lord as a reward. It is the Lord Christ you are serving. (Colossians 3:23–24)

─────────────── REFLECTIONS ───────────────

Instead of reflecting with questions today, I'd like you to use your reflection time to start your war plan for your children. Remember, it starts with a word from the Lord. Spend as much time as you need seeking God for this. Use the space on the opposite page to brainstorm a verse, mission statement, goals, and your nonnegotiables for your family or child. Once you have your idea, buy yourself a journal or create a poster board for each child. Whenever you can, pray over your children and the plans God has for them.

─────────────── POWER PRAYER ───────────────

Father, I thank You for _____. I thank You that You have great plans for my child's life. I ask right now that You reveal them to me. God, speak to me the way only You can. Lord, I ask that You empower me with wisdom and strategy to know how to get my child in line with Your vision. Let it be all about You and Your will. Show me, Lord, when I am in the way and when things need to be changed. Teach me to be humble and surrendered to Your will. I thank You, God, for Your plan over _____'s life, and I praise You for this child. Help me to stand firm in Your plan, no matter what happens in life. I trust You, Lord, that Your plans are good and perfect. Teach me to act on them without delay. I am believing for radical change in my home. May every attack of the Enemy against my child's calling be rendered powerless. In Jesus's name. Amen.

Chapter Four

OATH TO LOVE

Love recognizes no barriers. It jumps hurdles,
leaps fences, penetrates walls to arrive at its
destination full of hope.
MAYA ANGELOU

"Owe no man nothing but to love him."
I remember the first time I heard this phrase. In a church of about fifteen people, I thought, *Wow, this pastor has lost his mind. How offensive!* For some reason, this idea of owing no one anything but to love him or her made me wonder. In my mind, I considered my responsibility to be a good neighbor, care for those in need, forgive, pray for people, and even be a good member of society. Shouldn't we owe each other this? The phrase frustrated me so much, I went home irritated, wondering why this pastor would say such a thing. Within moments of my scholarly research on Google (insert giggle), it was evident that God agreed with the guy on stage. We are reminded by Paul in his letter to the Romans to "owe nothing to anyone—except for your obligation to love one another. If you love your neighbor, you will fulfill the requirements of God's law" (Romans 13:8 NLT).

After I swallowed my pride for being wrong and recognized the need to study my Bible more, I started to dissect this idea. How could this be? Aren't people entitled to more than this? Here's what God reminded me.

Love Is Enough

What I realized is that when we love the way God has called us to, it is enough. The God type of love that is patient, kind, doesn't envy, boast, or keep records is truly all we need. We don't have to expect more of ourselves or another. We don't have to have someone come through for us heroically or vice versa. Just love. And this travels down to our parenting as well. Love is what the next generation is watching for and responding to, wouldn't you agree?

When we love this way, we will find that all other things come into alignment. We will take care of the poor. We will forgive one another. We will treat others the way God would have us treat them. We will be loyal, honest, committed, patient, gentle, honoring, and more. I am convinced that anything more than loving a person God's way would put us in the position of pure idolatry toward another person.

Owe No Man Nothing but to Love Him

So what does this have to do with our motherhood journeys? Everything! We must be bold and unapologetic in our love toward our children and everyone else. Even those in the psychological community agree that love is the most important aspect of parenting. According to *Psychology Today*, "Love is the greatest tool for parents."[1] Researchers have found that those who come from homes characterized by love and warmth are more likely to have successful adult relationships, job satisfaction, and higher self-esteem. When we recognize that love is our primary responsibility, this is a game changer. I am convinced we've been sold a recipe for motherhood that was never intended by God. Our society has taught us that we have three jobs:

1. Raise children who are happy.
2. Train them to become responsible adults.
3. Try not to be the reason they need therapy later in life.

In doing so, we have become focused on creating memories, snapping pictures, enrolling kids in activities, and, around the teenage years, molding them into being upstanding citizens. I'm afraid that in the midst of our doing and doing and doing, we forget our primary responsibility: to love. As I continue, I pray not to offend you as the pastor once offended me years ago. Instead, I want to inspire you to recognize that love is far more important than any list of burdensome to-dos.

The One Thing You Owe Your Children

You don't owe your children explanations. You don't owe them shelter. You don't owe them yearly family vacations. You don't owe them the Christmas and birthday gifts they've been begging for. You don't owe them an allowance or the latest new phone. The only thing you are obligated to do is to love them. Mom, this should be a freeing moment if you really take it in. Leading with love inherently comes with responsibility.

Here is what this looks like in my life:

Because I love, I give food, shelter, and a listening ear without condition.
Because I love, I bring correction.
Because I love, I take the moment to reward when I feel it's necessary.
Because I love, I create opportunities for fun.
Because I love, I ask for forgiveness.

I do these things out of love for my children and a desire to honor God, not from a place of simply needing to make my kids happy. First Corinthians 14:1 (NLT) speaks to me each time I read it: "Let love be your highest goal!"

As you continue to read this book, I encourage you to take a moment to genuinely consider, without beating yourself up, how you love your children. Do you love them in a way that exemplifies 1 Corinthians 13 (the love chapter of the Bible) and 1 Corinthians 14:1? Do you love in a sacrificial way as God does? Are you gracious to forgive as only love can?

Here's a challenge. Ask any children you know what they love about their mothers. I can assure you their responses will be based on acts of love. Some children will say, "She takes care of me." Others, "I like how she listens to me." Few will say, "She gives me everything I want." It's how we care for our children that makes us stand out from the crowd. When others may dismiss them for their indiscretions or quirks, they can find acceptance and love from their mother. A mother's undying love can endure the hardest times because it's not rooted in or based on the child's behavior.

Love Should Reflect the Father's Heart

Let us not be so focused on checking the boxes of modern motherhood that we forget our primary responsibility: to love. In my heart, I find myself often using 1 Corinthians 13 to self-check how well I am reflecting the Lord's heart for my children. Let these words sink in as you read them.

> Love is patient, love is kind. It does not envy, it does not boast, it is not proud. It does not dishonor others, it is not self-seeking, it is not easily angered, it keeps no record of wrongs. Love does not delight in evil but rejoices with the truth. It always protects, always trusts, always hopes, always perseveres. (verses 4–7)

Years ago I spoke with a mother who shared her overall goals for parenting—how she believed her most important job was to raise her children to be respectful, God-fearing, intelligent adults. However, because this was her motivation, she was frustrated by how rule-driven her home had become. Her desire was to find the balance between allowing her children just to be joyful kids and training them properly.

This conversation was a reminder of the importance of leading with love. This mother is full of love for her children. In fact, I can personally attest that she is one of the most attentive and proactive mothers I've ever encountered. However, whenever we find ourselves more rule-driven than relationship-driven, a disconnect in relationship will eventually become evident. As mothers, we must allow our love rather than an outcome to be the driving motivation.

The importance of relationship is not a foreign concept to mature Christians. We understand that God wants us to follow His principles, but He also desires our hearts. Even more so, God goes out of His way to show His love for us. We see this clearly in the death and resurrection of Jesus Christ. As we start to take in the vastness of His love, we are drawn to Him even more. Just the idea of pleasing a God who loves us so much is enough to make us want to soak in all He instructs. Even when He brings correction, we know that it is out of His love for us. He is not a God with a whip trying to terrorize us into becoming perfect beings, but rather is a Father who loves us and wants the best for us. If God interacts with His children out of love, we should do the same.

Love like Jesus

There are countless examples throughout the Word exemplifying how God loves us. From saving the children of Israel from captivity, to dying on the cross, to leaving the Holy Spirit to guide us, He has proved that He loves us and is willing to do whatever it takes to show us. Yet although we know this, we can be left wondering how to go from knowing we should love like Jesus to taking practical steps to do so. Over the years, I've wrestled with how I can walk in this love from a genuine place without falling victim to just checking the boxes. I've found that one of the greatest examples of walking in love in the Bible is seen in Jesus's interactions with His disciples. If we look carefully, we can see clear patterns that we can use as a guide for our motherhood journey. Among other things, Jesus showed His love for the disciples in three basic ways: being consistent, being a source of comfort, and bringing correction. Let's take a few moments to investigate these.

Consistency

From the moment Jesus called His first disciples in Matthew 4:18–20, we see One who remained consistent. His first words to them were "Come, follow me . . . and I will send you out to fish for people" (verse 19). Interestingly, this never changes. His last words are remarkably similar, as He admonished His disciples to "go and make disciples of all nations, baptizing them in the name of the Father and of the Son and of the Holy Spirit, and teaching them to obey everything I have commanded you" (Matthew 28:19–20). Years later Jesus was still telling His disciples that He planned to send them out to impact the nations. Although they had spent countless hours together, gained new followers, and faced major adversities, the mission never changed. Jesus never wavered in His message to them. His ability to heal, and even how He spoke about the kingdom of God, was consistent. He said what He meant and meant what He said.

Consistency may be something we neglect as parents. Yet one way to create an atmosphere of love and care is to create a pattern of following through. In the *Psychology Today* article "Three Ways to Raise Secure Children," consistency is listed as a key element in raising children. The article states that when children are in a consistent environment, they "feel more comfortable and less threatened, resulting in a strong sense of security that will generalize to all aspects of their lives."[2]

Examples of inconsistent behaviors include bedtimes that are never the same, alternating between being strict and overly lenient, and telling children to behave one way while doing the opposite. When we respond or act one way on one day and completely shift the next, children are left wondering how their environment will change. It's important that we learn what works best for our families and keep it consistent. When we create consistent environments, we show that our love, much like God's, is intentional and purposeful.

Comfort

Another way Jesus showed love was to comfort His disciples. He knew they would face various trials, such as seeing Him be crucified, being persecuted by many, and eventually dying as martyrs. Yet His words were always the same: "Peace" and "I am with you." The same words that echoed throughout the Old Testament remained true as Jesus walked with His disciples. As mothers, we must be a place of comfort. On our children's hardest days, they should know they can find serenity and support from us. It is important that our children know they can run to us whether they have a paralyzing nightmare, aren't sure what to do next, or even encounter their first heartbreak. We should provide this kind of a safe place where they can always count on us for comfort in the hardest times. Even when we don't agree or understand their choices, our love for them should make us their safe place. The Lord created us as His arms on earth to comfort His children, pray for them, and remind them that He is always present.

The Lord created us as His arms on earth to comfort His children, pray for them, and remind them that He is always present.

Correction

As much as we are there for our kids on their hard days, the more difficult days for us are when we ask God to show us how to bring His correction and guidance in their lives. When you read the Gospels, you readily see that Jesus had no issue bringing correction. Whether addressing the religious leaders or His own followers, Jesus shared where He stood on different matters. He desired for those around Him to know the truth and walk in it. He knew that failure to address the disciples' lack of faith or doctrinal fallacies would make them vulnerable to attacks from the Enemy. He also knew that not correcting the religious leaders would lead many astray by their faulty thinking.

Although we will dive into discipline in chapter 10, I want to encourage you by saying that healthy discipline reminds our children that we love them and desire what's best for them. Whether we realize it or not, we understand this concept well. From not allowing your toddler to run across the street, to teaching your child not to touch hot surfaces, you know that failure to bring swift correction to a child facing imminent danger would be irresponsible. Some would say it's neglectful.

When we guide our children, we assure them that we care about them and want to do all we can to keep them safe spiritually, emotionally, and physically. Could there be any greater way to show love? If you want to be a mother who walks in strength, you must be willing to bring correction.

With this in mind, let's continue to discuss our role as warriors for our children. We are to be the squad leaders of the troops in our care. In a typical military setting, the squad leader reports to his or her command, mentors the troops, and ensures that the squad and the equipment are in good working condition. Yet before the squad leader reaches this career stage, there is something he or she must do. Every person who enlists in the US military must raise his or her right hand and complete the oath of enlistment:

> I, _____, do solemnly swear (or affirm) that I will support and defend the Constitution of the United States against all enemies, foreign and domestic; that I will bear true faith and allegiance to the same; and that I will obey the orders of the President of the United States and the orders of the officers appointed over me, according to regulations and the Uniform Code of Military Justice. So help me God.[3]

The oath of enlistment is not to be taken lightly. For many this is the start of a commitment that will last over twenty years to protect and serve their country. Today I want to ask you something radical. Would you be prepared to take an oath of service to the Lord? Not just for your children and their well-being—this oath would be about choosing to go all the way and to surrender your parenting completely to the Lord.

The reason we value and applaud our military is because we know that it's with great love that they risk their lives daily. We know it is their selflessness that motivates them to commit to situations that many would run from. At the basic level, whether you agree with the current mission of the military or not, the oath reflects the heart of Jesus: "Greater love has no one than this: to lay down one's life for one's friends" (John 15:13).

As a military spouse, I will never forget the first time I visited Walter Reed Bethesda Wounded Warriors pavilion. I was astonished by the many who had lost limbs in war. Although I knew some were saddened by what they'd lost, I was amazed by the many who found a strength they didn't have before. Many were thankful to be alive, but none seemed to regret being a proud member of the military. Their love for their country and for protecting others gave them the courage to push through the tough days. Needless to say, gathering around this community with love, meals, and support was the least I could do. When they took their oath of service, they meant it. Their bravery against the enemy and willingness to be selfless had become a badge of honor.

At this moment of your motherhood journey, you may feel defeated. You may relate to the soldier in that it feels like you have lost so much so far—whether you sacrificed your career to become a stay-at-home mom, work three jobs to provide, or have endured years of sleepless nights as you cared for your children. The weight of parenting may be a daily reality for you. I want to encourage you today: though you may feel like a battered soldier, you can stand tall because of your strength and stability that comes from the Lord.

You can look at the adversities thrown your way and love unconditionally. You can display God's heart even through the battles designed to take you out. In fact, every sacrifice you've made thus far has reflected the love you have for your children. You have loved not because someone told you to but because it wells up in you. And though you may feel like you want to give so many other things to your children, I want you to consider that when you love them as faithfully as you can, you *are giving them everything they need.*

It's easy to see love as secondary compared with other basic needs. But when you show your children the gift of love—through spending time together, listening, praying with them, and leaning in and hearing what they say and don't say—you leave them with an impression that can change their entire lives. You wipe up messes, you wipe where they've left crumbs, and you wipe away tears, but your dedicated love in action will stay in their memories.

Over the next few chapters, I want not only to speak life to your parenting journey but also to give you a strategy for loving your children on purpose. Let us start by making a commitment to no longer parent out of fear or the obligation to keep everyone happy, or in our own strength. Instead, let us allow the Father's heart to be our filter and our guiding light toward our children.

—————————— VICTORY VERSES ——————————

This is My commandment, that you love one another, just as I have loved you. Greater love has no one than this, that a person will lay down his life for his friends. (John 15:12–13 NASB)

—————————— REFLECTIONS ——————————

1. What do you feel like you owe your children?
2. Do you place an extra burden on yourself to ensure your children are happy and satisfied with you as a mother?
3. If you were to parent out of love rather than fear or your insecurities, what would be different about your parenting or behavior? Would you show more consistency, comfort, or correction?

—————————————— POWER PRAYER ——————————————

Lord, I need You to infiltrate my parenting. I thank You for the love and grace You have shown me. Even when I didn't deserve it, Your unconditional love has carried me through the hardest moments. On this day, _____ (insert date), I commit my life and parenting to You. I commit my will to You. I pray that You would help me carry Your heart when it comes to _____. Father, forgive me when I miss the mark. Help me go all the way and not grow weary in doing what would honor You. Teach me to bravely parent and love, even in the tough times. In Jesus's name. Amen.

Chapter Five

VICTORY MINDED

Victorious warriors win first and then go to war, while
defeated warriors go to war first and then seek to win.
SUN TZU, *THE ART OF WAR*

ONE OF THE MOST IMPACTFUL books on war was written by philosopher and military strategist Sun Tzu. Written in the fifth century BC, *The Art of War* shares approaches that are used by military leaders and entrepreneurs 2,500 years later. Concepts such as choosing your battles, leading by example, and timing is everything can be found nestled in this ancient text. Yet out of its many lessons, one major aspect that Sun Tzu lists as a key to overcoming an enemy is that every warrior must have a victorious mindset. According to Sun Tzu, before the battle has ever begun, you must be confident that you can and will win. A warrior who goes into war with expectations of defeat will make poor choices, be unprepared, and cause others to stumble.

When it comes to life, there are two kinds of people: those who expect the worst and those who expect the best. Many Christians find themselves in the first category. They may know the Word and even turn to prayer often. Yet when things happen, they simply *hope* it all works out. They lean on phrases like "Everything happens for a reason" and "All things work together for my good." Although both are true, we can sometimes unintentionally turn these powerful promises from God into passive phrases that quickly leave us victims of our circumstances.

When it comes to our children, we must be careful not to fall into this trap of *only hoping* God will work things out. If we aren't careful, rather than standing in faith and expectation that God will fight on our behalf, we can find ourselves overwhelmed and wondering if God will ever answer our prayers. Before long, instead of fighting in prayer for our children, we become defeated and afraid of the devil. Take a moment to take that in—children of God, the King of Kings and Lord of Lords, being terrified of the devil! This should seem like an oxymoron to you.

Because we belong to Jesus, we are poised to win every battle before it even starts.

We have no need to run or cower from the Enemy. We must remember that because we belong to Jesus, we are poised to win every battle before it even starts. In the worst-case scenario, if we were to lose our lives, we would still get to be with the Lord for all eternity. This is why the Bible reminds us, "Where, O death, is your victory? Where, O death, is your sting?" (1 Corinthians 15:55). Whether in life or in death, we win! We can be victory minded, if for no other reason than because we know the promises we find in His Word. We must go into every battle we face knowing *we* win!

We win because God never leaves us or forsakes us (Deuteronomy 31:6).

We win because God loves us so much, He decided we were worth dying for (John 3:16).

We win because He is in control (Proverbs 16:9).

We win because He knows all and sees all (Daniel 2:22).

We win because He gives wisdom to his children (James 1:5).

We win because nothing can separate us from the love of God (Romans 8:31–39).

We win because Jesus died on the cross and conquered hell, death, and the grave!

This should cause us to rejoice! Yet although "we win" is a great notion to hold on to, until we believe it *and* act like it, we will never see God's best for our lives and our children's lives. One of the greatest tragedies I witness daily is Christians who walk overwhelmed and in expectation of the worst-case scenario. They say things like, "God moves for other people but not for me" or "Things never really go right for me." I have even heard Christians declare such notions as, "My mama and grandmother died from it, so I will too." I often ask myself, *What good is it to be a Christian and not expect God to move on your behalf?* One of the benefits of Christianity is the reassurance that we serve a God who cares about our most intimate needs and answers when we call. Unfortunately, we can reach a point in our Christianity where we lose hope and stay stuck in defeat, wondering if God is present in our time of need.

Although it's not an easy feat, if we want to change the way we parent, we must first change how we think. Our thoughts can either be grounded in God's truth or in the deception of what we *believe* is true. This could be because we've seen it work out this way in the past or haven't known anything different. Our thoughts are often filtered through our own ability and what we can physically see. This becomes much more apparent when we've failed or we *feel* that God has disappointed us.

Today I want to encourage you to no longer allow defeated thoughts or ideas to take residence in your mind. In 2 Corinthians 10:5 we are commanded to "take captive every thought to make it obedient to Christ." Taking a thought captive requires us to pause and ask ourselves, *Is this thought from the Lord, or does it contradict His Word or character?* We must also ask ourselves, *Why would God want us to think or act contrary to His Word?* In other words, it's not about our perspective but His! Every thought must be filtered through God's love and truth.

The Influence of Thoughts

In His infinite wisdom, God created the human brain with the capability of rewiring, accommodating, and releasing chemicals based on the physical need or even thoughts of the individual—a phenomenon known as *plasticity*. Studies have found that people who focus on positive thoughts have greater plasticity. Joy-filled thoughts lead to greater focus, more creative thinking, and the ability to understand and navigate more complex scenarios.[1] In other words, a person's thoughts can create a sort of self-fulfilling prophecy. If you see good things, your brain responds accordingly.

The medical community is also aware of the power of thought. Numerous studies have found that patients given a placebo respond similarly to those who have been given real medication. For some people, the simple act of believing that they are healed causes the brain to respond accordingly.

Conversely, researchers have examined brain imagery of those who struggle with negative thoughts, namely, anxiety, fear, and depression. Negativity has been seen to cause decreased function in the cerebellum, leaving individuals with a lack of focus, poor coordination, and other physical ailments, including increasing one's chances of developing dementia.[2] Yes, how we think matters from the inside out! Before we fight any battle on the outside, we have to address the war within our own minds. Sadly, some have spent so many years swamped in negative thoughts that their brains wouldn't have it any other way—they have reset themselves to accommodate their expectations. My prayer today is that this is not your testimony.

For many years I lived a life plagued by defeated thinking. I had become accustomed to thinking that God wasn't aware of my struggles with parenting. I wondered how I could ever be a good mother. I would find myself feeling like the day-to-day struggles were too much for any person to manage. And although I knew the Word and God's promise to be with me, I felt like I was parenting alone. During these times, my days were filled with constant frustration, as I screamed my way through parenting and apologized often for my angry outbursts toward my children and my husband. I cannot count how many times I hid in a closet in tears, wondering how I could ever be good enough or live up to the image I had been portraying in public. I had become a victim to the constant war within my head. The Enemy had spent years highlighting my every insecurity, and I had bought into the lies. More than my children's unruly behavior or my own parenting mistakes, my hopeless, defeated thoughts took the lead of my parenting journey.

I am living proof that we must become keenly aware of how we think and the influence this will have on our parenting. I want to pause and show you the difference between a person who operates from a state of defeat and one who stands in great expectation of God's power. The following chart is an example of how we can take a defeated thought captive and filter it through the truth of God's Word.

DEFEATED THINKING	VICTORIOUS THINKING
I'm a bad mother.	I am a mother in need of God's grace daily.
I can believe for other people but not for myself.	If God can do it for them, He can do it for me.
I will probably fail.	I will do my best with God's help.
I will never be healed.	By His stripes I am already healed.
I can't pray aloud—the devil may hear me.	My God has already defeated the Enemy.
I'm going to brace myself for the next attack.	No weapon formed against me shall prosper.
I am not enough.	In my areas of weakness, God is strong.

Defeated thinking focuses on what I can or cannot do in my own strength. Victorious thinking is centered around the limitless power of what God can do. As mothers, we must consider what thoughts we've allowed to take control. If we aren't careful, we'll find that our thoughts will lead us to parent from a place where we are insecure, angry, resentful, timid, and doubtful that the Lord is on our side, much like I was years ago.

A Look at Moses

Out of all the biblical characters, Moses gives one of the clearest pictures of how our thoughts can hinder or empower. When you think about Moses, you may envision the hero of the Old Testament. Perhaps you imagine him boldly entering the courts of Pharaoh and demanding, "Let God's people go!" Maybe you consider his triumphant victory over the Egyptians as he led the children of Israel through the Red Sea, which then covered and killed all those who tried to keep them captive. It may even be Moses's leadership in the wilderness or his conversations with the Lord that led to the creation of the Ten Commandments that come to mind. Whatever you associate him with, many theologians agree that Moses serves as the Old Testament's best illustration of Jesus's heart, ability to rescue, and leadership of those who were spiritually immature.

Although Moses's life is seen as heroic, his story begins with the man wallowing in self-doubt and defeated thinking. In Exodus 3 we see God's initial beckoning of Moses. While shepherding in the fields, Moses had an unusual encounter with an unconsumed burning bush and the voice of the Lord speaking to him for the first time.

> "Do not come any closer," God said. "Take off your sandals, for the place where you are standing is holy ground." Then he said, "I am the God of your father, the God of Abraham, the God of Isaac and the God of Jacob." At this, Moses hid his face, because he was afraid to look at God.
>
> The Lord said, "I have indeed seen the misery of my

people in Egypt. I have heard them crying out because of their slave drivers, and I am concerned about their suffering. So I have come down to rescue them from the hand of the Egyptians and to bring them up out of that land into a good and spacious land, a land flowing with milk and honey— the home of the Canaanites, Hittites, Amorites, Perizzites, Hivites and Jebusites. And now the cry of the Israelites has reached me, and I have seen the way the Egyptians are oppressing them. So now, go. I am sending you to Pharaoh to bring my people the Israelites out of Egypt." (Exodus 3:5–10)

Needless to say, the words "I am sending you" probably echoed throughout his mind in surround sound and caused immediate panic and fear. You see, Moses was not perfect. In fact, he was a murderer, a stutterer, and a person who was nervous to lead. When approached by the Lord, his initial response was not one of joy and acceptance of this honorable call. Let's look at Moses's responses to the Lord:

- But Moses said to God, "Who am I that I should go to Pharaoh and bring the Israelites out of Egypt?" (Exodus 3:11).
- Moses said to God, "Suppose I go to the Israelites and say to them, 'The God of your fathers has sent me to you,' and they ask me, 'What is his name?' Then what shall I tell them?" (Exodus 3:13).
- Moses answered, "What if they do not believe me or listen to me and say, 'The LORD did not appear to you'?" (Exodus 4:1).
- Moses said to the LORD, "Pardon your servant, Lord. I have never been eloquent, neither in the past nor since you have spoken to your servant. I am slow of speech and tongue" (Exodus 4:10).
- But Moses said, "Pardon your servant, Lord. Please send someone else" (Exodus 4:13).

It's clear that although Moses recognized who God was, his fear of not being believed, his stuttering issue, and his feelings of insufficiency made him recoil from God's master plan. His inner thoughts reminded him of what he couldn't do rather than what God could do. In the natural sense, the notion that Moses could say *anything* that would convince Pharaoh to release what is believed to be at least hundreds of thousands of slaves is seemingly impossible. When confronted with this battle, I can't help but imagine that most of us would have echoed the same sentiment: "Excuse me, Lord. Can you choose someone else?" Fortunately, Moses didn't remain in this place of defeat throughout his journey.

By Exodus 14 we see Moses finding a renewed sense of confidence and leadership. After what appeared to be a victory, Pharaoh finally released the Israelites, and we find Moses in a daunting scenario. However, no sooner than Pharaoh allowed them to go, he changed his mind and chased after the Israelites, who had just begun to walk away from Egypt toward freedom. In a perilous scene, Pharaoh and his army advanced toward the children of Israel full of fury and refusing to release those whose labor was a central part of the Egyptian economy.

As you can imagine, the Israelites looked to Moses in terror at the possibility of being trapped again by the enemy. In front of him, an impassible raging sea. Behind him, a sea of people he had been called to lead, with Pharaoh and his army ready to overtake them. With no clear instruction of what to do, Moses had a choice—succumb to the enemy or trust God like never before. His choice would mean the difference between victory and defeat, freedom and slavery, for generations to come. Rather than run and cower, Moses acted on his belief that God could save them. "Then Moses stretched out his hand over the sea, and all that night the LORD drove the sea back with a strong east wind and turned it into dry land. The waters were divided, and the Israelites went through the sea on dry ground, with a wall of water on their right and on their left" (Exodus 14:21–22).

With a lift of his hand, Moses believed and acted in faith that God would deliver. And God, as He always does, responded. As mothers, we must know in the depths of our souls that God has a plan, and when the opportunity arises, we must move fearlessly. Though we may feel pressed by the Enemy or face a situation that seems impossible to pass, we can trust that the Lord will act as we move in faith. But before we can act on God's words, we must first believe them.

There are three valuable lessons from Moses's story that can empower us to shift our thinking as mothers.

1. We must remember what God has already done.

A mindset shift happened within Moses from the burning bush in Exodus 3 to the Red Sea miracle in Exodus 14. In chapters 5–14, we see ongoing conversations between God, Moses, and Pharaoh. Throughout this time, a pattern is created—the Lord instructing Moses on his communications with Pharaoh, Pharaoh refusing to budge, and the Lord instituting plagues on the Egyptians. These plagues included boils, locusts, flies, and even the death of the firstborn of the sons in Egypt. Yet while havoc reigned throughout the Egyptian kingdom, God protected the Israelites. With just a word, God showed Moses and everyone else that He was completely in charge.

When it comes to our own lives, we must remember where God has brought us from. Take a moment and think on the lowest point of your life. Perhaps you've been rejected, very ill, or betrayed, or you suffered from the consequences of your own actions. Maybe you were told you couldn't have children, but the Lord blessed you with a child or gave you the opportunity to adopt one. Maybe the Lord provided for your family during a financial crisis with exactly what you needed and more. Whatever the case may be, was it not the Lord who was with you and helping you to walk through these moments? Our history with God is what empowers us to step courageously into every battle. If He has already provided for you in the past, then you know He will do it again. He doesn't just do something once and leave you to fend for yourself afterward. It may look different than you expect, but God will move on your behalf.

2. We must keep our eyes focused on God, not on the circumstance.
When faced with overwhelming thoughts, we must keep our eyes focused on the Lord rather than allowing ourselves to be plagued with the what-ifs or to fear the battle ahead. In the initial encounter of Moses in Exodus 3, we see a man who was second-guessing everything the Lord said. Not only did he fear Pharaoh not believing him, he also worried about the repercussions associated with standing toe-to-toe with a person of such power. With each plague, Pharaoh grew more and more frustrated with Moses and imposed harsher work on the Israelites. Even the Israelites found themselves angry with Moses for all that was happening. Yet Moses continued to pursue the Lord's instruction. He was aware that this was a battle he couldn't fight on his own. Pharaoh's words and attacks were irrelevant in comparison to God's plans.

As mothers, we must do the same. From the beginning of time, the Enemy has been trying to trip up God's people. Yet those who are victory minded know that God has always been successful. Even when you flip to the end of your Bible, you will find that the devil does not have the final say. Our role is to keep our eyes on the Lord no matter what the Enemy says or how tough the opposition. For example, suppose a mother learns that her child has been diagnosed with a rare illness. She could spend hours on Google researching the disorder, start seeing herself as a failure, and get angry with God for not looking out for her child. Before long her thoughts could become inundated with regrets, worry, and worst-case scenarios. In doing so, she would cause herself more turmoil and be unable to encourage her child, who needs her the most. Instead of taking this self-defeating route, the wiser thing would be to look to God for His strength and direction. And although the outcome may vary, she can stand firm on the knowledge that God's promises are *still* true and He is *still* good. If we remain focused on the battles and our own ability, we will never walk in true victory.

3. Our thoughts must reflect God's promises.
In Moses's first encounter with God, a key phrase was spoken by the Lord: "I have come down to rescue them."

"So *I have come down to rescue them* from the hand of the Egyptians and *to bring them up out of that land* into a good and spacious land, a land flowing with milk and honey—the home of the Canaanites, Hittites, Amorites, Perizzites, Hivites and Jebusites" (Exodus 3:8, emphasis added).

Before any of the plagues took place or Moses uttered his frustration to Pharaoh, God had had a plan for rescue. Before the sea was parted, the Lord had spoken His promise. God's words to Moses were clear—He heard the need and would handle the situation by any means necessary. Thus, anything that happened after these initial words, "I have come down to rescue them," was to put the Israelites in prime position for God to show His glory and victory. Although it may not have felt like it to Moses and the Israelites, God was at work to fulfill His word every step of the way. Moses's job was to trust God and follow His word. God's role was to fight and win on their behalf, which we clearly see throughout Exodus and, even now, in our own lives.

Our Why

Whether we believe it or not, we are much like Moses. We've been entrusted to carry our children to their destiny. Like the children of Israel, our children may not have the faith or time with God to be strong on their own. They need a leader who is firm in her belief that God can do the amazingly impossible on their behalf. Take a moment and reconsider the chart from page 67. I want you to focus on the defeated column and pause. From one mom to another, can you imagine if your child thought like this? What would you say to your child? Would you come into agreement with them that his or her life is on a downward spiral, validating the thoughts, or would you offer your child hope and the message of God's truth like we find in the second column? Here's the bottom line: if we want to see our children walk in courage, we have to do so as well.

We have to know God's words and let them reverberate within our hearts so that whenever the Enemy speaks words of deception we can say, "Not today, Satan!" Jesus said it like this: "My sheep listen to my voice; I know them, and they follow me" (John 10:27).

Remembering Who God Is

There are three final things about the God we serve that will help to reframe your thought life.

- Our God is omnipresent.

  God doesn't operate within our understanding of time and space. He can be at all places at any time. He doesn't split Himself in millions of pieces to be distributed around the world. Instead, *all* of who He is, is present at all places at any given moment. He is as present with you as you read this book as He is with a teacher in Greenland, a child in Haiti, and an elderly person at a nursing home in Germany.

- Our God is omniscient.

  He knows everything. There's no thought you can think without Him knowing about it. There's nothing that catches Him by surprise or leaves Him speechless. He knows what happened from the beginning of creation and what will happen until the end of time. In fact, He is the source of all knowledge itself. As the Bible says, He knows the beginning from the end (Isaiah 46:10)

- Our God is omnipotent.

  He is all-powerful. In other words, there has never been and will never be anyone or anything with more power. He is not limited by what others would deem impossible. He doesn't work within human limitations. His power supersedes what we could ever imagine or wrap our mind around.

Warrior Mother, it's high time we lean into who our God is! I want to ask you a hypothetical question. What if I told you that someone is planning to break into your home tomorrow? After your initial onset of shock, what if I told you a few more key things? Number one, I will be watching over you the entire time. Not only will I see you, but I will also see the robber from miles away. To make the odds even better, I tell you that I know his exact plan for breaking in and what he plans to take from your home. For good measure, I reassure you that no weapon he brings into the home can harm you and that I have all the power needed to protect you at any given moment. No matter what happens, just trust that I'm watching over you, believe that I have a plan, and know that nothing will be lost. Better yet, when it's all over, the assailant will wish he never entered your home and will leave defeated. All you have to do is believe what I have said and do what I instruct you to do when the times comes.

Chances are strong that you would feel confident tomorrow. You would know that you have someone on your side who has your best interest in mind and who knows every detail. The entire scenario would be rigged in your favor. This same victorious mindset must follow us as we journey into becoming mothers who champion our children. We have a God who knows every attack the Enemy will try to wage on your family's life, and God has perfectly positioned you to win every time. When it comes to our thinking, we must take the reality of who God is seriously. Yes, we serve a God who is all-knowing and all-powerful in all things, and who can work mightily in every situation.

Going back to the story of Moses, it took time and intentionally seeking God for his needs, but eventually Moses came to recognize that it would be his reliance on God that would pave the way for victory. Moses's choice to conquer his thinking would help lead an entire nation to freedom. Had he remained focused on his own insufficiencies, past, or what seemed an impossible feat, he would have cheated himself out of being a part of one of the greatest miracles. Today, allow your faith to be the foundation of your thoughts and actions. Anything less will keep you and your family in a cycle of worrying before every battle and being more focused on the opposition than God's Word. Your children need you to be as mentally and emotionally strong as possible for the battles to come.

Think victoriously.
Trust the Lord.
Approach each battle knowing you've already won.

———————————— VICTORY VERSE ————————————

Finally, brothers and sisters, whatever is true, whatever is noble, whatever is right, whatever is pure, whatever is lovely, whatever is admirable—if anything is excellent or praiseworthy—think about such things. (Philippians 4:8)

———————————— REFLECTIONS ————————————

1. Referring to the chart, do you tend to be more defeated in your thoughts or victorious? Share an area of your life where you feel victorious.
2. In 2 Corinthians 10:5, we are told to take our thoughts captive. Let's practice this by naming three lies about yourself or God that you've allowed yourself to believe. Find a Bible verse that contradicts each one of them. What does knowing these verses do for your faith?
3. In what ways have you seen your thoughts positively and/or negatively impact your children's lives?

———————————— POWER PRAYER ————————————

Lord, I praise You for knowing all and being in every situation. God, I ask that You help me to believe. If there is any offensive thought in me or way that doesn't line up with Your truth, expose it to me. Help me recognize patterns where I've allowed the Enemy's voice to resonate in my life more than yours. God, I pray that every neurological pathway that's been created due to my own doubt, fear, and feelings of inferiority be restored back to its original state. I pray for complete healing of my mind and restoration of my thoughts. Help me to walk victoriously into every battle knowing that You are my God, and You fight every battle on my behalf. I trust You, Lord, for my own life and for my children's lives. Teach me to empower them with Your truth and to teach them how to reject everything that doesn't come from You. I choose to no longer believe, receive, or accept any thought that does not glorify You. In Jesus's name. Amen.

Chapter Six

SQUARED AWAY

And yet in our world everybody thinks of changing
humanity, and nobody thinks of changing himself.
LEO TOLSTOY, *WAR AND PEACE*

SHOW UP ON TIME AND be presentable.

I will never forget my first day at Spelman College. Our first order of business before stepping into any classroom was to attend the mandatory new-student orientation. In a room full of former high school valedictorians and salutatorians, the speaker reminded us with a stern face, "To be early is to be on time, to be on time is to be late, and to be late is never acceptable." When she finished this, she paused and uttered these words: "And look your best when you do it."

The students were quickly taught that the school meant business. The professors would lock the doors five minutes *before* class started, and coming to class with pajamas on was frowned upon. As women of Spelman College, we were to set the standard of excellence and present ourselves the way we wanted to be treated. If we wanted to be treated with honor and valued in our future careers, we had to look and act as such. This has stuck with me to this day. Being on time is like being five minutes late for me, and showing up to the grocery store without at least a pop of eyeshadow and a nice outfit is seen as a petty crime in my book.

Thus, when my husband joined the military, the heavy emphasis on his military attire was no surprise. Just as my college expected students to look and act their personal best, the military had high standards. From head to toe, every aspect of a military member's uniform had to be squared away, or perfectly in order. During a routine uniform inspection, soldiers must make sure that the ribbons on their uniforms are straight, their faces are clean-shaven, their hair is the appropriate length, and their uniforms fit correctly. Soldiers must even ensure that they have on appropriate socks. Being properly dressed is about more than simply looking respectable, as it was at my college; a military member's failure in this area could lead to other issues when in training or in battle.

Recently I had the opportunity to speak with Major Jon Harvey of the National Guard about why being squared away is so important. According to Major Harvey, being prepared keeps everyone from getting hurt in war. "The wrong uniform can be life or death for you and everyone else. Your feet will freeze without the right boots, and someone will need to rescue you. The uniform shows your teamwork and your discipline. One team, one band, one sound." In other words, one person's failure to be prepared or to follow the uniformity required could affect an entire squadron.

Check Yourself

Have you ever felt the weightiness of showing up to motherhood feeling unprepared? As mothers, we hold a heavy responsibility. I am afraid that so often we consider how we can fix our children and help them thrive yet forget that we must be mentally and spiritually clothed for success. Unless we are properly squared away in how we think, behave, and follow the Lord, those following us (our children) will struggle as well. I realized many years ago that sometimes our biggest enemy is "In-A-Me." Many times we become our own stumbling block when we fail to address the issues that may be underlying our own lives. We make the devil's job easy when we fail to take a self-inventory. So although we may desire to be victorious for our children, we are victims of our own addictions, insecurities, and poor choices.

The hard question for us today is this: What are we clothing ourselves in? If you did a true inspection of your heart and mind, what would you find? Would doubt function as your helmet, leaving you to question every promise of God? Would fear be a patchwork coat, causing you to make careless choices? Are you wearing confusion and division as shoes, making you a magnet for gossip and unsure of your decisions? Would comparison be your glasses, making it difficult to appreciate the life that God has given you?

Warrior Mother, what you clothe yourself in will directly impact your ability to lead, especially when challenging times come. In my life, I have seen this unfold firsthand when my daughter was diagnosed with epilepsy. As I mentioned in chapter 2, her seizures ignited a panic I had never experienced before. Within a week of her diagnosis, I had spent well over a thousand dollars (that we didn't have) in monitoring equipment so I could watch my daughter day and night. On the outside, these actions may have appeared like good parenting. But the truth is that how I responded was merely a symptom of the paralyzing fear I was suffering from since childhood. For years prior, my phobias were immense and included being afraid of dogs, riding in a car alone, clowns, being robbed, death, crossing the street, and speaking in public. These fears were debilitating, and at some points I would have considered myself a "fearaholic." In my mind, having these fears kept me safe from making careless choices and made me cautious.

Fear had become my place of safety. And although I hid it well, when I faced the battle of my daughter's illness, my areas of weakness were exposed. Instead of showing up as a warrior on her behalf, I behaved as one who had been wounded by fear for many years. My lack of trust in God to take care of *my* everyday needs was now spilling over into my lack of trust that He could care for my daughter in her illness. The hysteria I caused about her epilepsy during those years spread like a cancer to the entire home. My daughter was constantly worried about her condition. My husband and other children spent their days exhausted by my franticness and were even ignored, as all my attention was on this one issue that had reignited my fear. My fear affected everyone involved.

I am certain I am not alone. So often these areas of insecurity come to the surface when battles arrive, and we aren't mentally or emotionally stable enough to handle them. Just as with military members, failing to take a self-inventory can affect everyone involved. Being a mother requires us to walk in self-awareness. Failure to do so will cause us to walk in self-deception and distort our perception of reality. One of my favorite verses on this matter is found in the Psalms: "Search me, O God, and know my heart; test me and know my anxious thoughts. Point out anything in me that offends you, and lead me along the path of everlasting life" (139:23 NLT). Here's the truth of the matter: if we refuse to accept that we may be a part of the problem, we can't be a part of the solution.

In this chapter, I want to challenge you to go a little deeper and ask yourself if there is anything in your life that is causing you to stumble. One of the Enemy's greatest tricks is to deceive us into thinking we are just fine the way we are. This is worse when we have qualities that may make us look like good Christians. We may check off the boxes by going to church weekly, praying for a friend, or even making a meal for someone in need. However, when no one is around, what sound reverberates in our hearts? What do we carry that may be offending the Lord? When we fool ourselves into thinking that we are perfect, we walk in self-deception and can expect very little growth personally or in our motherhood. Until we confront our shortcomings, we certainly will struggle to give grace for anyone else's. "So, if you think you are standing firm, be careful that you don't fall!" (1 Corinthians 10:12).

The Enemy's Tactics Exposed

As Christian mothers, we should remain in a place where we desire to be more like Christ. In fact, often when I feel like I am in a beautiful place in life spiritually, an unexpected situation, such as a death, betrayal, or disappointment, comes in to remind me that I am still standing in the need of prayer. I struggle with feeling rejected, deal with isolation, and even find myself wrapped in fear from time to time. So although we will never be perfect, we have a duty to seek the Lord to evaluate any thought or behavior that may be a stumbling block to us or our kids. I want to spend a few moments highlighting what the Enemy attempts to clothe God's children in on a regular basis. Let's take a moment to be self-reflective and see how these traps of the Enemy have a direct impact on how we parent. And remember, when God shows us a part of ourselves that needs correction, it is for our growth, not to shame us.

Doubt

Doubts can make us "unstable in all our ways" (James 1:8 NASB). When we struggle to trust God daily, we give access to the Enemy to sow seeds of doubt. Before long, small doubts can turn into an outright belief that God doesn't love us or care about us. We see doubt introduced from the beginning when Satan asked Eve, "Did God really say?" in Genesis 3:1. As we see with Eve, one seed of doubt can have a domino effect where we find ourselves influencing others and ultimately where our relationship with God suffers. The Enemy uses doubt as a hook to cause us to wonder if God is *really* present, *really* listening, and *really* able to do all He says. Doubt in parenting is infectious, as it causes our children to question our faith when hard times come. If we want to set an example for our children, we must combat every thought of doubt with a promise from God's Word. We will discuss this more in the next chapter. But it is wise to listen to the words of James on this matter: "But when you ask him, be sure that your faith is in God alone. Do not waver, for a person with divided loyalty is as unsettled as a wave of the sea that is blown and tossed by the wind. Such people should not expect to receive anything from the Lord. Their loyalty is divided between God and the world, and they are unstable in everything they do" (James 1:6–8 NLT).

Regret

The Enemy loves it when people remain in shame, regret, and guilt. This trap makes us feel like we will never be good enough. Regret causes us to see our past as the reason we are stuck. Instead of focusing on God's redemptive power in our lives now, our minds constantly wander to our poor choices from years ago. We say to ourselves, *If I would have done this* or *If I could have just said that* or *If I didn't have this child, my life would be different now.* Mothers who had their children at an early age or out of wedlock often project their lists of regrets onto their children. We see the regrets show up in the unbearably strict parent who refuses to allow her children to make the same mistakes and even the mother who forces her child to play a sport or instrument to live out her own dreams. Not only is the mother miserable, wishing she were doing the things of her dreams, but the child has to constantly live up to the pressure of fulfilling the mother's dream. The Enemy uses regret in parenting to influence a mother's mind with thoughts like regretting the birth of a child, wishing she could just run away, or worse, that she wasn't alive at all.

Regret untamed can lead to major depression and cause children to feel as if they are a burden. We can rest assured that although we have all made mistakes and have things that we wish we could have done differently, God's grace for us is bigger than our circumstances. We can rest assured that we can run to Him with a sincere heart and find healing for these tough matters over time and through prayer. "Therefore, there is now no condemnation for those who are in Christ Jesus" (Romans 8:1).

Addiction

Often when we think of addiction, we immediately picture a drunkard, a crack-addicted homeless person, or someone gambling their life savings away. However, addiction can show itself in many ways that we often don't think about. You can be so addicted to food that you gorge yourself and feel horrible about it later. If you have a shopping addiction, you can find yourself spending all your family's money with little left to save. Perhaps you are addicted to social media and spend hours watching other people's lives but fail to take care of the daily needs of your home. I have been guilty of this! Whatever the case may be, we can find ourselves trapped in a cycle of knowing we should stop something but being unable to find the strength to do so. In many ways, this addiction becomes a form of idolatry. Before long we seek out our vice before we seek God. When we are sad, we run to it. When we are excited, we must have it.

If we aren't careful, our addictions can easily replace God and cost us financially, spiritually, and physically.

Without a doubt, most people will face addiction at some point in their lives. As mothers, we must take inventory of the habits that keep us from being fully functioning moms. Sadly, when we are trapped in addiction, we spend an enormous amount of time and energy on our vices. Taking care of our homes or spending time with our children becomes secondary compared with doing what makes us feel good in the moment. This trick from the Enemy keeps us distracted and inattentive to what may be happening in the world around us. Learning self-control in areas that may have kept us bound for decades is not easy but very necessary.

There is no stronghold too heavy for the Lord to help us out of if we are serious about changing. Breaking free from addiction will require an abrupt change in some areas and saying no to others and even to ourselves concerning the temptation at hand. Remember, anytime we choose something or someone over God repeatedly, this is idolatry and may be a sign of an addiction that must be uprooted. I love what Paul said about our ability to overcome any and every addiction: "No temptation has overtaken you except what is common to mankind. And God is faithful; he will not let you be tempted beyond what you can bear. But when you are tempted, he will also provide a way out so that you can endure it. Therefore, my dear friends, flee from idolatry" (1 Corinthians 10:12–14).

Pride

If you think you are the best at everything and have all the answers, you may struggle with pride. A prideful person is normally defined as someone who talks about themselves a lot or likes to be the center of attention. Yet, like addiction, pride can be subtle. It can come in the package of one who is judgmental or critical of other people. In their own way, prideful people have a pattern of looking down on people who they deem aren't on their spiritual or emotional level. Even a parent can be susceptible to treating her child as a lesser person simply because the child is younger. This form of pride can be hard to spot, as parents should have authority but not to the point that it insinuates that the child's thoughts are insignificant.

Quite frankly, if we allow ourselves to be prideful in parenting, we won't seek God for our needs because we will have fallen into the trap of thinking we have it all together. Thus, even if God sends a warning about an area we need to change, our own inclination to be right and not wanting to be corrected will lead us to ignore God's voice.

Prideful people think they know better than even God Himself but can expect destruction everywhere they go (Proverbs 16:18). A mother's pride can lead her to be stubborn, sarcastic, degrading, and pretentious toward even her children. Since children learn by example, we must know that this is not God's best for our children. How dangerous pride can be if we allow it to reign in our homes. Knocking down pride starts with you and me stopping to evaluate whether we have allowed ourselves to be clothed with this unbecoming trait. While the Word is clear that pride leads to self-destruction, the Word also offers us a better path. "When pride comes, then comes disgrace, but with humility comes wisdom" (Proverbs 11:12).

Rejection

Struggling with rejection may not seem harmful initially. However, fear of rejection will cause you to become paranoid in your relationships. It will cause you to avoid making deep relationships. Fear of rejection will result in your being unable to accept God's Word for yourself. In fact, whenever something goes wrong, you will process the painful situation as proof of your own inadequacies rather than seeing the reality of the situation.

As one who desires to parent in strength, you must not allow fear of rejection to reign in your life. I have seen mothers who struggle with the fear of rejection inadvertently reject their own children. Although it is not their intention to do so, their inability to see themselves as worthy of love blocks their ability to love well. Here are some subtle signs that rejection may be affecting your life and parenting.

- You struggle to tell your children no for fear of them not liking you.
- Embracing your children feels uncomfortable.
- When you are not acknowledged, you feel angry.
- You are a people pleaser.
- You try not to make big decisions for fear of getting them wrong and being ostracized.
- You feel like you will never be a good enough mother.

The Enemy will use rejection to torment us if we allow it. He knows that if he can cause us to be overly worried about what people think and how they perceive us, we will become paralyzed. Instead of making bold choices and doing what God has called us to do, our fear of not being loved and accepted will keep us in a state of compromise.

If we live to try to make other people happy, we will always be disappointed.

In my own life, I experienced this for years. I struggled to say no, was furious when I felt left out, and would do anything to be a part of the crowd. This cost me my sanity, relationships, and friends. In my effort to people please and be accepted, I actually pushed people away, as I had become a friend that required 100 percent attention. Thus, the cycle of rejection never ended. The bottom line is this: if we live to try to make other people happy, we will always be disappointed. Whenever our lives become wrapped up in other people's acceptance versus God's truth, we'll be flustered and feel rejected. This is dangerous ground for mothers, as we will find ourselves allowing our own children's opinions to become our driving force, to keep them happy. Remember, our only responsibility is to love them! If we want to be warrior mothers, fear of rejection must be prayed out of our lives and replaced with the truth of God's Word about who we are and what actually matters.

Fear

Fear is one major tactic of the Enemy. It was fear of missing out that caused Eve to eat of the forbidden fruit. It was fear of losing authority that caused Pharaoh to throw the Israelite boys into the Nile. It was the fear of death that caused Peter to deny Jesus three times. Over and over throughout the Bible, we see that fear causes people to make careless choices.

At the foundation, fear is the emotion that causes us to believe that God is not in control and cannot handle our current circumstances. In today's times, fear comes out in the form of anxiety, panic attacks, depression, and isolation. What started as simple doubt about a circumstance can internalize and be the source of sleepless nights, irregular heartbeats, stomach issues, and a heaviness that cannot be easily shaken. An influx of anxiety may be rooted in hormonal imbalances, poor nutrition, brain disorders, or even too much caffeine.[1] In other cases, anxiety and fear are the result of a spiritual attack. Fear is a weapon used by the Enemy to bring torment and is not of God. The Bible reminds us that our loving God doesn't pass out fear to His children and that those who continually walk in fear may need to strengthen their trust in the Lord. "There is no fear in love. But perfect love drives out fear, because fear has to do with punishment. The one who fears is not made perfect in love" (1 John 4:18).

Every time a paralyzing fear arises, we know that the Enemy is at work. Because fear is not from God, we have complete authority to tell it to *go* in Jesus's name. This act of casting out fear and every thought that is not of God will take great intention but will be vital for us as Christian mothers. We combat fear not only by saying the name of Jesus but also by making a conscious effort to eliminate anything that may be adding to the fear we are experiencing. Here are a few examples:

- Constantly internet researching the worst-case scenario for a medical diagnosis.
- Watching movies that pertain to death, the demonic realm, and any other area that makes you feel uneasy spiritually.
- Allowing people to speak negatively or express doubt about God's ability to help you in a situation.

Every time we find ourselves clothed in fear, we must ask ourselves, *Is there anything I may be doing to come into agreement with the fear?*

In our efforts to keep our kids safe, fear-based parenting may lead us to make many mistakes. From being so overprotective that our children hardly ever interact with people outside our homes, to giving our children everything they desire for fear that they may feel unloved. Over time, fear-based parenting leads children to feel unsure and unconfident about making choices. Those who parent in fear will inadvertently teach their children not to trust God and will become a stumbling block to their child's spiritual growth. God's heart is that we would not be nervous about every aspect of our child's life but that we would trust Him in every way. Today I pray that you would ask yourself, *Are there any ways I have allowed fear to be in the driver's seat of my parenting?* Instead of allowing fear to dictate our parenting, let us run to the Lord when we feel afraid or unsure of what to do next. He is a good God and will answer when you seek

Him. "I sought the LORD, and he answered me; he delivered me from all my fears" (Psalm 34:4).

Comparison

The last area I want to shed light on is comparison. The Enemy uses this device as an opportunity to sow seeds of jealousy and covetousness. In a time in which we are constantly exposed to other people's lives through social media, thoughts of comparison can happen multiple times in one day. I've found myself spending hours on social media comparing my weight, my children, and my accomplishments to other women. The constant stream of other people's highlight reels made my everyday life seem dull and caused me to wonder if God had forgotten about me.

On the surface, it appeared everyone had it together but me. This comparison drove my career choices, caused me to stress about the appearances of myself and my children, and kept me in a state of striving to have more titles and recognition. I spent years exhausting myself trying to be like people whom God never called me to be. A good rule of thumb is that you will always fail when trying to live out someone else's calling. It took me years to reach the point where I was confident enough in God's sovereign plan not to be envious when it seemed like someone else's life was better than my own.

Here's the thing about this sneaky ploy of the Enemy. Comparison causes us to think God is not good and plays favorites. Yet when we allow comparison to be our lens for viewing the world around us, this is our personal way of saying, "God, what You have given me is not enough." As mothers, we've all seen this concept firsthand, from the ungrateful child on Christmas morning to the siblings who compare what they have been given with the others in their home. In the same way, when we walk in comparison, we struggle with being content. Reaching a place where we can be thankful about what God is doing for us in this season will help us to be better parents overall. If we want our children to walk in contentment, we must model contentment for them.

Dressed for Success

How, then, can Christian mothers clothe themselves for success? Many Christians are aware of the spiritual armor discussed in Ephesians 6. Paul encourages us to walk out our faith in recognition of the battles ahead against the evils of this world (seen and unseen). Every Christian, male or female, should wear this metaphorical armor as if their life depends on it. Let's take a moment to look this over.

> Put on the full armor of God, so that you can take your stand against the devil's schemes. For our struggle is not against flesh and blood, but against the rulers, against the authorities, against the powers of this dark world and against the spiritual forces of evil in the heavenly realms. Therefore put on the full armor of God, so that when the day of evil comes, you may be able to stand your ground, and after you have done everything, to stand. Stand firm then, with the belt of truth buckled around your waist, with the breastplate of righteousness in place, and with your feet fitted with the readiness that comes from the gospel of peace. In addition to all this, take up the shield of faith, with which you can extinguish all the flaming arrows of the evil one. Take the helmet of salvation and the sword of the Spirit, which is the word of God. (Ephesians 6:11–17)

With the belt of truth, we keep ourselves reminded of God's Word. This belt is what holds all other pieces of the armor in place, and without truth we can expect to be easily conquered by the Enemy. The breastplate of righteousness guards the heart and reminds us to walk in obedience to keep ourselves safe. On our feet, we stand in peace and recognition of the gospel as our foundation. The shield of faith keeps us ready and able to deflect every lie and attack of the Enemy. Our faith keeps us from the effects of the attack. The helmet of salvation is what covers the mind and reminds us that what Jesus

Christ has done for us is our ultimate victory, no matter the battle. And finally, the Word of God is our sword, which is powerful enough to destroy a ploy of the Enemy. The Word is sharp and can tear through every stronghold but is also sensitive enough to dissect and operate on our hearts when they are damaged. This armor is meant for your personal protection and alone is enough to keep you covered for life against any and every attack.

Now I want to draw your attention to other clothing Paul spoke of in the book of Colossians. The Colossian church was known for having great faith and love. Yet they struggled with knowing what traditional Jewish rules to follow and how to follow Christ amid a changing world. Paul reminded this small group of believers how to walk in a way that would honor the Lord, putting off all things that caused distraction and unrighteousness. A lifestyle that depended on fleshly needs, inner strength, or happenstance would cause issues in their witness for Jesus. To truly live a lifestyle that reflected their faith, they needed to have a different way of doing things.

Listen to what Paul told the Colossians:

> Therefore, as God's chosen people, holy and dearly loved, clothe yourselves with compassion, kindness, humility, gentleness and patience. Bear with each other and forgive one another if any of you has a grievance against someone. Forgive as the Lord forgave you. And over all these virtues put on love, which binds them all together in perfect unity. (Colossians 3:12–14)

Warrior Mother, the aspects that Paul shared here are like the accessories to our spiritual armor. You see, the armor Paul discussed in Ephesians 6 reflects how we can personally protect ourselves from spiritual attacks. But in Colossians, Paul changed the outlook and encouraged us to be mindful of how what we carry can be a blessing to others. As we end the chapter, I want to take a few moments to lean into how compassion, kindness, humility, gentleness, patience, and love will become the perfect attire for us to parent with God's heart.

Compassion

Jesus walked and ministered with compassion. Compassion is the insatiable desire to be aware of another person's pain and to make their situation better. Jesus had compassion throughout the Gospels as He healed the woman with the issue of blood, fed the hungry thousands, and raised Lazarus from the dead. Jesus was never too busy to stop and act.

As mothers, we should offer compassion—from holding our preschooler close when they fall rather than just telling him or her to shake it off to recognizing when our older teens may need a break from chores to finish their schoolwork. Compassion is when we lend an ear to hear our child's heart, even when we disagree with their stance. Those who walk in compassion choose to look beyond their current circumstances and seek to serve other people, even when inconvenient. "The LORD is gracious and righteous; our God is full of compassion" (Psalm 116:5).

Kindness

Kindness and compassion sometimes overlap. Kindness is about being intentional. Whether through a random act or purposeful seeking to help others, you can be kind at any moment. Whereas compassion denotes a genuine need for help, kindness can be seen as being nice (just because). You can operate in kindness simply by putting a nice note or piece of candy in your child's lunch box. Reminding your teen how much you appreciate him or her is another way you can be known for kindness. What a blessing we can be to our children by finding intentional moments to simply show kindness. Although this may not seem like a warrior move, I can assure you that when your children encounter their toughest battles, they will remember how intentional you are. This, my friend, will make you a safe place that they can run to.

Humility

Much like the Enemy desires to cloud our judgment with pride, God wants us to see the world through the eyes of humility. Yet being humble is a choice. When we put other people above ourselves and don't allow ourselves to believe we are more significant, more spiritual, or more deserving than others, we walk in true humility. In parenting, humility allows us to admit when we are wrong and to seek forgiveness when needed.

Being humble also means a willingness to forgive other people. In our pride, we can believe that the other person is undeserving of *our* grace. This is not only hurtful to the other person but insulting to the Lord, who forgives anyone willing to ask. Paul wrote, "Be completely humble and gentle; be patient, bearing with one another in love" (Ephesians 4:2).

Gentleness

Gentleness is the quality of being soft, tender, and mild mannered. The gentle person chooses to be delicate and full of grace in tough situations. Rather than answer in a brash manner or without reservation, mothers who walk in gentleness make a choice to be the calm in the storm *and* to pause before they respond. "Let your gentleness be evident to all. The Lord is near" (Philippians 4:5).

Patience

We all know that patience is a central aspect of parenting—from waiting on children to finally follow an instruction to believing God for a healing on their behalf, to putting up with a whiny child at the grocery store, we must learn to be calm when frustrated. A lack of patience can lead us to make hasty choices or to behave in ways that we later regret. We must clothe ourselves in patience. What helps me is to remember that the Lord has been patient with me for so many years. When I doubted Him, when I walked away from church, when I made the same mistakes over and over, He still loved me. He still drew me in. If God, the perfect One, could extend such patience to me, who am I not to do the same for others? Remembering this keeps me mindful that my goal is to model the Lord in my parenting, even in the difficult moments or when I feel annoyed.

Love

Paul finished this section by telling the Colossians to cover themselves with love. Interestingly, he told them not to wear love only but to put love on top of compassion, kindness, humility, gentleness, and patience. I see the imagery of the small child in an oversized winter snowsuit. We have all seen pictures of little ones bundled from head to toe in this puffy attire. It's as if the suit is dictating how the child walks, talks, and moves. No matter how much they want to, the child simply cannot get away from his or her snowsuit. This should be our reality when it comes to being completely covered in love. Love should be the first thing our children and the world see. It should dictate how we move and interact, even when its uncomfortable. I want to say that one more time. Love should dictate how we move, act, speak, talk, and care for others, even when its uncomfortable. Walking in godly love will not always be easy and requires us to think before we speak and put others before ourselves, but it's always worth it.

I leave you with these final words of Major Jon Harvey: "If the army wanted me to have it, they would have issued it to me in my rucksack." Anything we need for battle, God has already given us access to. Every other thing we choose to accept from the Enemy will leave us unable to fight the battles ahead. Let us put off every stronghold that binds us and put on the character of Christ, walking in full humility, patience, and love. Refuse to show up to your next battle improperly dressed for the occasion.

——————————— VICTORY VERSES ———————————

Search me, God, and know my heart;
   test me and know my anxious thoughts.

See if there is any offensive way in me,
and lead me in the way everlasting. (Psalm 139:23–24)

———————————————— REFLECTIONS ————————————

In lieu of the normal reflection questions, end this chapter with a moment of transparency before the Lord. As you answer the following questions, ask the Lord to show you your heart on these matters and reveal any way the Enemy has clouded your perspective with his untruths. After you do so, use this week to ask God to show you portions of His Word that speak truth to these areas.

- Do you see God as distant or close?
- Is your past a hindrance or a source of strength?
- Do you perceive yourself as confident or uncertain?
- Are you more joyful or sorrowful about motherhood?
- Do you parent out of love or fear?
- Do you have any addictions or forms of idolatry that need to be removed?
- Have you allowed fear of rejection to be your lens for how you parent or interact with others?
- Do you see motherhood as an opportunity or a chore?

———————————————— POWER PRAYER ————————————

Lord, I come to You humbly today. I ask that You search me. If there is any area of my life that's causing me to stumble, open my eyes to see it. Lord, I repent for the sins of _____ that have been a distraction and have hindered my walk with You. I want to be better for myself and for _____. I need Your grace daily. God, show me if my filter for parenting has been affected by my own insecurities or fear. Show me how to parent in a way that brings You glory. Lord, I ask that You help me to be clothed in compassion, kindness, humility, gentleness, patience, and love. Let these things be what I carry with me into parenting. Forgive me for when I have allowed anything else to guide my interactions. Help me to see motherhood as a privilege and not a burden. Renew my joy, and show me how Your hands are guiding my journey. Give me strategy to be set free from the habits that are affecting my life and how I parent. I give You complete permission to take the lead in my life. Speak, Lord, I'm listening. In Jesus's name. Amen.

Chapter Seven

WAR OF DECEPTION

Be alert and of sober mind. Your enemy the devil prowls
around like a roaring lion looking for someone to devour.

1 PETER 5:8

DURING MY TIME IN MIDDLE school, I was an emotional punching
bag for bullies. Being a scrawny big-eyed teen with a voice so high-
pitched it would make Mickey Mouse cringe made me an immediate
target for mistreatment. As much as I tried to fit in, I was reminded
that I was simply not up to par. I quickly learned that my bullies' primary goal was to damage how I viewed myself and break my spirit.
Their method of attack was always the same—to call me out and to
find other people to do the same. My days on the playground were
full of hurtful words being thrown at my appearance and character. I was "ugly and stupid," with eyes that were apparently too big,
clothes too outdated, a voice too squeaky, and legs too skinny.

Each day I heard these words, I believed them more and more.
The truth is, if bullies could get me to doubt my worth, they would
have me exactly where they wanted me. There was no true need to
push me in the mud (although they did) or physically fight me. If they
could get into my mind and cause me to doubt myself and fear them,
they had me right where they wanted me.

With little effort on their part, I would remain defeated and never
be strong enough to stand up for myself. Before the next interaction

with them would occur, I believed I wasn't strong enough, beautiful enough, or worthy to win against them. This mental cycle of being put down and putting myself down kept me in their tight grip. Into adulthood, I found myself still believing their words. I had been deceived by their lies for so long that it had become my truth. This is what deception does.

Much like my middle school bullies, the Enemy loves to use deception. We see his lies in the Bible from the garden of Eden to Judas in the New Testament. Time and time again, the Enemy tries to convince God's people to doubt the truth. The Enemy is relentless in his pursuit to cause you to doubt God's Word, His promises, and His power. Unfortunately, the devil will use absolutely anyone to accomplish his mission. He will use a parent to speak doubt into a child's self-worth. He will use a teacher who is unfriendly or dismissive of a child. He will even use an unfaithful spouse or a jealous sibling to impart lies. Just like a school bully, the Enemy will gather as many people as he can to gang up on you.

Knowing Your Enemy

I cannot emphasize enough the gravity of the spiritual battle we are in. This next section is not for the faint of heart or those who are not ready to see their personal and parenting lives shift. Sadly, many Christians go to church every Sunday having no idea there is an unseen world that is active all around them. Just like there is a natural world we can touch, see, and experience, there is a supernatural realm that has a strong influence over much of what we deal with daily. I believe we try to ignore the spiritual realm because it makes us feel uncomfortable, and somehow we convince ourselves that it's not a big deal because we have Jesus. Yet Paul says, "Our struggle is not against flesh and blood, but against the rulers, against the authorities, against the powers of this dark world and against the spiritual forces of evil in the heavenly realms" (Ephesians 6:12).

Although many modern-day Christians tend to ignore this aspect of life, we're walking in deception if we refuse to believe there are real demons and that Satan is a powerful entity. His ability to persuade, influence, and oppress is not to be ignored. This doesn't mean we should be afraid, as all power and authority have been given to Jesus. However, we must recognize that there are satanic powers at work that keep us bound and that influence our thinking—and that we need to be set free from. The great news is that if you are a child of God, the devil cannot take possession of your thoughts or make you do anything. He can only influence through things like thoughts, other people, and media.

Former satanic leader John Ramirez, in his book *Unmasking the Devil*, describes his time in the occult:

> The first thing you need to know about the spiritual being called Satan, or the devil, is that you won't find him running around in a red suit, with horns and a pitchfork. He won't come at you with bared fangs dripping blood. No! He would much rather you fall for the lie that he is just a myth and he doesn't exist at all. But if he can't convince you to swallow that, his next move will be to invade your life with all the hidden powers of hell, unseen but deadly.[1]

Warrior Mother, we need to be very aware of the real influence of the devil. Remember, even Jesus had interactions with demonic forces during His time on earth. So much so that He taught His disciples how to cast out demons and to heal people. Often the modern-day church praises the miracles of Jesus but neglects to point out that He also delivered people from the oppression and possession of demonic spirits. "Jesus called his twelve disciples to him and gave them authority to drive out impure spirits and to heal every disease and sickness" (Matthew 10:1).

Yes! The disciples were not only taught to bring forth healing, but they were also keenly aware that there were demonic forces that held people captive. For those who want to believe that this only occurred during the times of the disciples and is no longer relevant, look at what Jesus stated *after* His resurrection: "And these signs will accompany those who believe: In my name they will drive out demons" (Mark 16:17).

If we fail to realize that many of the battles we face are not because of a specific person disliking us or because of the actions of an unruly child but because there is a real Enemy, we will only touch the surface of winning the battles the Enemy sends our way. One of the Enemy's greatest deceptions is causing Christians to believe that he is not real and that he has no power. We can look at the book of Revelation and see quickly that the devil and the demonic realm are real and active even now.

Let's be clear—as a child of God, you cannot be possessed or fully controlled by the Enemy, because the Holy Spirit dwells within you! Possession by a demon implies complete ownership of the individual. I believe this is the case with those who enter a school and kill children or those who have absolutely no regard for humanity. These people will often say, "The voices in my head told me to do it." Praise be to God—if you are a true believer, this will never be the case. However, you can still be oppressed (under attack) and be dealing with the Enemy's influence daily. This was evident when Jesus spoke to Peter, who was clearly a follower but was still susceptible to not following God's voice completely and even denying Jesus. He said, "Simon, Simon, Satan has asked to sift all of you as wheat" (Luke 22:31).

Friends, anyone has the potential to be influenced by the demonic. If we say to ourselves, "Well, I accepted Jesus, so I'm good," please reread the above verse. Peter knew who Jesus was more than any other disciple but was still impacted by the spiritual realm. Unfortunately, many believers are dealing with the effects of the presence of unclean spirits of lust, bitterness, jealousy, strife, or rejection and have no idea where their troubles are coming from. Pastor Tony Evans of Oak Cliff Bible Fellowship says that too many Christians have lost sight of demonic forces that act as "a spiritual mafia that attacks us in the spiritual and brings about our pain in the physical."[2] Although I am a firm believer that not every circumstance is the result of demonic forces, there are times when we may be facing a full frontal attack from the Enemy and be unaware. There is a reason the apostle Paul sternly warned to "not give the devil a foothold" when discussing spiritual warfare (Ephesians 4:27).

Unfortunately, we give a foothold, or open the door of our lives, to the devil unknowingly by speaking negative words over ourselves, watching movies laced with demonic themes and witchcraft, reading tarot cards, using chakras, trying to talk to family members who have passed away (side note—demons often parade as a deceased family member to gain access to your life), eliciting sexual behavior, and gossiping, among many other things.

Here are some signs you may be under a spiritual attack:

- Irrational fear
- Debilitating anxiety
- Bouts of uncontrollable anger or violence
- Compulsive behavior (addictions, unbiblical sexual behaviors that you struggle to stop, eating disorders)
- Hearing unexplainable voices
- Bitterness (obsessiveness over an offense)
- Demonic nightmares or encounters
- Extreme weariness (unable to function or focus, especially when interacting with Scripture)
- Unsettling response to the name of Jesus or the Bible (feeling sickened when entering a church)

In other words, some behaviors and actions are a sign of spiritual forces at work and not just a bad habit or personality issue. My prayer for you today is that your eyes will be opened to see if some of your current woes may be a spiritual attack more than anything else. If so, I highly encourage you to speak with the leaders of your church, who can pray with you and help you to break free from these strongholds. Much like we must be self-aware and squared away, we must also be sensitive to discern when something may be a spiritual issue. Having this recognition will help you to have a sense of awareness when you may be under demonic attack.

So what does this have to do with motherhood? Everything! We see that demonic forces can easily affect your entire being. If demons can attack you, don't be so naïve to believe these same entities can't have influence over your children. One needs only to turn on the television to see how children are being bombarded with witchcraft, unbiblical sexuality, vulgarity, profanity, and more to see that the Enemy is doing all he can right in front of our eyes. From the ads in between innocent programming to curriculum taught in school to bring confusion, mothers must be more vigilant than ever when it comes to what their children are exposed to. Unless we are overwhelmingly intentional about every single interaction, every piece of media they are exposed to, children will be subjected to worldly influences daily. The Enemy is simply not playing fair when it comes to attacking their lives.

I want to reiterate that not every negative circumstance is caused by demons. I am a firm believer that Christians cannot use the devil as their scapegoat for every poor choice. Many sicknesses (mental or physical) aren't because a person let the devil in. Some are because you ate unhealthily your whole life and developed a disorder, your hormones are imbalanced, or you don't care about living a righteous life in any capacity. Let's not give the devil all the credit—some aspects of what we experience are the result of a fallen world, our sin nature, or life's circumstances. Other things, however, require us to take responsibility and own our choices to go against God's Word. On judgment day, you won't be able to say, "Well, God, I tried my best, but that ole devil *made* me drink till I passed out, cuss out my children, and ignore Your Word altogether." If you do, I'm sure you will be greeted with a response from our heavenly Father that you won't like. As a parent, can you imagine if your child gave you the response "the devil made me do it" every time he or she behaved inappropriately? Needless to say, you would still hold your child accountable for his or her actions.

This is where prayer comes in. If we are truly unsure whether what we are experiencing is a spiritual attack, we can seek God. Even more so, we have the right as Christians to do just as Jesus spoke to the disciples, to "cast out demons" in His name. I cannot count how many times I have had to pray with boldness and tell the devil to "GO!" from my house. One instance occurred when my fourth child was suffering debilitating nightmares. I cried out in Jesus's name that the spirit of fear and every form of demonic activity leave my dwelling place. Sure enough, after months of night terrors, he was suddenly free. Years later this same child falls asleep faster than any other child in our home. This is just one of many examples in which I have seen a frustration be solved by a prayer for Jesus to rid my home of demonic influence. Prayers of deliverance are powerful tools for Christians, and we shouldn't be afraid to stand boldly on the Word of God. Our God is greater than every demonic force. Let us remember this as we face these moments in our parenting: "If the Son sets you free, you will be free indeed" (John 8:36).

Psychological Warfare

The Enemy often attacks us through psychological warfare. When we think about this from a historical military standpoint, this form of warfare isn't as direct as dropping a nuclear bomb or ambushing an enemy. Yet psychological warfare, also known as propaganda, can be just as deadly. A slight twist of the truth, a pointing out of a potential flaw, an exaggeration or outright misleading can cause nations to be turned upside down. This tactic involves influencing a person's mind, behavior, and motives to believe what the enemy desires. In fact, in war an enemy force will know that their method of psychological warfare has been successful if they can get their opposing force to confess and alter their behavior accordingly. Let me repeat that phrase so you can soak it in. In a war, if the enemy can get you to confess an untruth and change your behavior, he knows the warfare has been successful. Does this sound familiar? The Enemy of our souls does the exact same thing. One twist of

God's Word will cause you to suddenly start speaking things that are untrue and have you acting in ways that go completely against the Word of God. Is this not what we saw in the garden of Eden with Eve?

Psychological warfare was used by Hitler during the Holocaust. According to the Holocaust Museum, Nazi powers were able to infiltrate every aspect of culture from film to art to music to newspapers. The Nazis were able to cause many people to believe that the Jews were the real enemy, only after sex and money.[3] By perpetuating this idea, more and more people believed it and were able to ignore the atrocities that ensued during the Holocaust. A lie that originated from the evil of one man's heart spread like wildfire, killing six million Jews and five million non-Jews.

This is a notable example of how one lie from the enemy can affect not just the person but entire families and cultures. The Holocaust reminds us, to a greater extent than any other story, that we must be careful about what we listen to and believe in our homes.

As Christian mothers, we have a responsibility to be aware of how the Enemy attempts to deceive in even subtle ways. The apostle Paul said to be alert "in order that Satan might not outwit us. For we are not unaware of his schemes" (2 Corinthians 2:11).

Again, the goal of psychological warfare is to cause you to confess what the enemy desires and for your behavior to be altered. A bonus victory for the enemy is for you to teach others (like your children) to believe the misconceptions. Below is a list of common ideas that the Enemy uses to infiltrate the believer's mind.

LIES OF THE ENEMY	GOD'S TRUTH
God didn't really say that.	God does not lie or change His mind. Numbers 23:19
How can a good God do that?	God is a good God, yet we live in a fallen world, which means we will face trials. James 1:17

LIES OF THE ENEMY (CONT.)	GOD'S TRUTH (CONT.)
How could God or anyone ever love you?	God loved you before you were even born and intricately knit you together in your mother's womb. Psalm 139
Could God really forgive you?	God is merciful to forgive. Psalm 103:12
Of course that happened to you!	God has good plans to give us hope and a future. Jeremiah 29:11
How can you expect anything good will ever happen to you?	God is fighting for us, and we can stand in faith that He is taking care of us. Exodus 14:14
What's the point of even trying?	God gives us strength through the good moments and the difficult moments to try again. Philippians 4:13–14
Does God even speak to you?	God reveals Himself to His children in an intimate way so that we may know the path to take. John 10:27
You deserved to have that happen to you.	Although we will encounter difficult times, we are able to stand firm, knowing that tests and trials help us to grow deeper in the Lord. James 1:2–3
That sin isn't that bad.	When we know what we should do and do the opposite, or when we sin without regard, this is displeasing to the Lord. God's Word holds the final say on what is sinful. Galatians 5:16–21

The truth is, the Enemy uses propaganda every chance he gets. He will do all he can to distort how we see God and influence how we interact with His Word. He is so ruthless that he doesn't go easy because a person is a child. If we struggle with negative thinking, low self-worth, doubt, and fear, we are fooling ourselves to believe that our children may not also be under spiritual attack. Oftentimes we'll look only at poor behavior and get frustrated. We may not understand why they won't just do the right thing or be good. Yet we never know the level of psychological warfare they may be experiencing themselves. This is why we must always keep ourselves and our children covered in prayer, for we never know the spiritual battle that may be ensuing.

Paul reminds us of the importance of not allowing our minds to come under siege by the Enemy's propaganda. "Do not conform to the pattern of this world, but be transformed by the renewing of your mind. Then you will be able to test and approve what God's will is— his good, pleasing and perfect will" (Romans 12:2).

If we want to overcome the psychological warfare tactics of the Enemy, we must renew our minds. Renewing our minds is intentional and requires us to purposefully reject every lie the Enemy speaks. When we find ourselves feeling defeated, we must assess if we have believed a lie of the Enemy, been guilty of confessing those lies, and changed our behavior accordingly. These are sure signs that we have fallen victim to psychological warfare. We must renew our minds by praying, reading God's Word, and taking authority over every thought.

Renewing the Mind with Prayer

Prayer, which we discuss more in chapter 8, is the foundation of our Christian journey. Without purposeful prayer, we can expect that we will never win in the battlefield of the mind. Prayer goes beyond simply reciting a routine plea or praise; it is an enthusiastic conversation with the Lord. What a blessing to have a direct connection with the Author of truth! Could there be a better person to answer our questions or clear up any confusion from the Enemy? If you haven't already scheduled a time to specifically pray for yourself, your child, and the world around you, stop reading and do so *now*! If we want to renew our minds, we must be quick to pray. Pray like your child's life depends on it—because it does.

Renewing the Mind with the Word

The Word of God is your spiritual blueprint for success. Reading the Bible should be a part of your daily life not because you *have* to but because you *get* to. In other words, we can't just say we want our minds to be resolute on God's Word but not know what the Word says. Finding Scriptures to hold on to, searching the Word for stories of overcoming, and learning God's commands can only benefit us. As we learn to stand firm on the Word, we can also teach our children how to do the same. When they face difficulty with bullies, we can draw them back to David and Goliath. When they feel a task is too big for them, we can remind them of Noah building the ark. When they struggle with forgiveness, the story of Jesus asking the Father to forgive the very crowds who had crucified Him can be our answer.

Knowing the Word not only refreshes us but gives us wisdom to know how to navigate the schemes of the Enemy. I find that the more I read God's Word, the more it comes alive for me—teaching me how I can trust God and walk in joy no matter what the circumstance. Thus, when the Enemy tries to persuade me, I've spent so much time in God's Word, my foundation is secure. I cannot be shaken, because I choose to believe His words over the fake news of the Enemy. I know God's words because I have resolved to read them, to write them, to say them aloud, to sing them, and to even cry them out in my time of need. Hallelujah! There is victory in knowing the Word down deep in your soul. "I seek you with all my heart; do not let me stray from your commands. I have hidden your word in my heart that I might not sin against you" (Psalm 119:10–11).

Renewing the Mind with Authority

Another major aspect of renewing your mind is to take authority over every thought not in accordance with God's Word. To do so, you must come to recognize the Enemy's voice and God's voice. It has been said that God's voice, the devil's voice, and our own all sound the same in our heads. But here's what I know to be true—God's voice is unlike any other. He only speaks truth. Thus, one clear sign that the Enemy is speaking is if the thought that passes through your mind is a lie, suggestion, exaggeration, or a twist of Scripture. Remember, the devil is the father of lies. He cannot speak truth, and his goal is to kill, steal, and destroy you and your child by any means necessary. If he can get you to doubt God's Word, great. If he can get you to hate yourself and your life, perfect. If he can get you to believe that God doesn't exist or care about your circumstance, ultimate victory. When we become aware of the Enemy's voice versus God's voice, we can recognize the Enemy from a mile away when he is influencing us or our children.

GOD'S VOICE	ENEMY'S VOICE
Life	Death
Truth	Deception
Encouragement	Discouragement
Motivating	Nagging
Constructive	Critical
Kind	Mean-spirited
Reflects Christ's love	Reflects the Enemy's character
Sincere	Manipulative
Forgiveness	Aggravation
Patience	Bitterness
Adds	Takes away
Builds up	Tears down

Lies We Believe

Our thought lives matter. The Enemy can cause much harm through a simple suggestion, for thoughts are one of the most powerful aspects of the human experience. As we saw in the example of Hitler, thoughts without regulation can affect the lives of many. The well-known proverb says it best: "Your beliefs become your thoughts. Your thoughts become your words. Your words become your actions. Your actions become your habits. Your habits become your values. Your values become your destiny."

Simply put, thoughts become beliefs and beliefs become actions. Whether we like it or not, our thoughts transform our lives for good or bad. Our job as mothers is to thwart the Enemy's plan to destroy the thought lives of our children by acting as buffers between his tactics and their minds. The more we can inspire them with the truth of God's Word, the better.

If we are not careful, the lies of the Enemy can infiltrate the mind of a child and cause that child to feel inferior. We see this in the psychological experiments by Kenneth and Mamie Clark in the 1940s, a time when Jim Crow laws and segregation were prevalent. Known as the famous "Doll Test," the two researchers used over three hundred African American children, ranging from three to seven years old, to study prejudices and low self-esteem in young children. With four dolls who were identical except for skin color, researchers questioned the students using various phrases, such as, "Show me the nice doll," "Show me the bad doll," and "Show me who you would play with." Throughout this study, the children tended to answer similarly. The darker dolls were seen as the bad ones and the ones least likely to be played with.[4] Needless to say, many of the African American children ended the study with tear-filled eyes.

The thoughts and beliefs of the community about their race had infiltrated their own young minds. Much like the Germans were influenced by the propaganda concerning the Jews, these children had fallen victim to the psychological warfare the Enemy uses. They had been convinced by society that they were of lesser value and internalized the lie, and their behavior began to mimic the deception. The "Doll Test" is a perfect example of how a child as young as three can believe they are unwanted and unloved. This is why we must be aware and counterattack every lie of the Enemy concerning our children immediately!

We mothers are not exempt from falling prey to this war of deception. How many times have we believed that we are failing at motherhood or unworthy of love? How many times have we questioned if God was *really* good or if He was *really* able to help us? Over and over again, I have learned that the Enemy will use anyone and everyone to bring in thoughts of inferiority and defeat. It is up to us to see the lie for what it is and cling to our God when these moments arise.

Knowing Who You Are

Just like my middle school bullies, the Enemy attacks our identity. Many times the Enemy slips into our thought lives and emotional states because although we *know* the Word, we struggle to apply it to ourselves. Our inability to truly see ourselves as God's children, whom He absolutely loves, gives the Enemy access to our thought lives. Before long we will allow doubt, fear, comparison, and regret to overtake us. Until we come to accept who God says we are, we will never walk into the fullness of God's plan for us. The Enemy knows that if he can get us to second-guess God's words over us, we will show up to every battle insecure. But today, I want you to say this aloud: "I am who God says I am."

> Our inability to truly see ourselves as God's children, whom He absolutely loves, gives the Enemy access to our thought lives.

I want you to get excited about who you really are in Christ. You see, the only reason the Enemy is able to wreak havoc in your life is because you have believed his propaganda. It's time we break free from every lie and walk into God's truth about us, for our sake and our children's sake. How can we teach our children to break free of the Enemy's lies when we are still bound ourselves? Jesus said it like this: "Can the blind lead the blind? Will they not both fall into a pit?" (Luke 6:39).

I pray that your eyes will be opened to God's truth about you. I want to take a few moments to tell you who you really are. As you read these four aspects of your identity in Christ, imagine yourself as a member of a sports team in a huddle just before the big game against your greatest rival. Try to feel the excitement of the coach telling you that you are a winner and that you have everything within you to overcome your adversary. Whenever you find yourself falling victim to the Enemy's deception, remember this and get pumped up! Own these truths and carry them wherever you go. Every time the Enemy tries to attack you with his common tactics, remind him of who you are.

Take it a step further—teach your children these same truths so they can withstand the Enemy's attacks. Allow me to be your personal victory coach over the next few minutes with these truths from God's Word. Feel free to replace the words "You are" with "I am" as you read about who you are.

1. You Are God's Masterpiece.

Yes, you are God's masterpiece! You are not a mistake. You are not an accident. You were created on purpose to do great things in this earth. In Genesis 1 you find that you are created in God's likeness and that He takes delight in you. In Psalm 139 you see that God intricately made you. Your originality, strengths, and talents reflect the uniqueness of who God is. There has never been and never will be a person who can walk out God's call for your life the way you can. You are designed by the King of Kings and the Lord of Lords. There is beauty in your story and in your growth. You are not an accident or a product of happenstance. No matter who your mother or father is or the conditions of your childhood, your life matters. Just as God spoke to Jeremiah, He called and appointed you for a great work (Jeremiah 1:4–5). You are His masterpiece. And guess what—so is each child in your care.

2. You Are Chosen.

God chose you. In His loving-kindness, He called you. In Romans Paul declares that while you were yet a sinner, Jesus chose to die for you. He chose you to be a significant part of your children's lives. He chose you to share the gospel with them. He chose you to dwell with them as a walking, talking testimony for all to see. Though many in life may have rejected you, you have a God who sees you in your frailest moments and still calls you His own (Isaiah 43:1). You are accepted by the Father and handpicked to do all He has called you to do for His glory.

3. You Are Loved.

God loves you so much, you were worth dying for. His love for you cannot be denied, taken away, or trampled. Nothing can separate you from His love. Romans 8:38–39 states that "neither death nor life, neither angels nor demons, neither the present nor the future, nor any powers, neither height nor depth, nor anything else in all creation, will be able to separate" you from the love of God. Even when you struggle to love yourself, God loves you. This love is not conditional or easily swayed. It is dependable. His love doesn't disappoint or discourage but carries you through every situation.

4. You Are Forgiven.

God has forgiven you. Although there is nothing you could do to possibly deserve His forgiveness, He forgives you anyway out of His great love for you. He does not dwell on your past mistakes or constantly remind you that you have failed. Instead, Psalm 103 says that as far as the east is from the west, so He has removed our transgressions. In His greatest act of forgiveness, God saved our souls from eternal tragedy. No matter how much the Enemy tries to convince us that we are unworthy or unloved, the death and resurrection of Jesus Christ is our reminder that God's forgiveness is for us.

Warrior Mother, the battle of the mind is something we will deal with all the days of our lives. Yet we can stand strong knowing that the Enemy will only have as much power as we allow. My prayer for you is that you would recognize the signs of when the Enemy is at work in your home. Whether he is attacking through psychological warfare and the telling of lies about who we are or through demonic oppression, we can be free when we find help from the Lord, who has already won the victory over the devil. Let us stand up to the devil boldly with the Word of God and with authority.

VICTORY VERSE

Submit yourselves, then, to God. Resist the devil, and he will flee from you. (James 4:7)

REFLECTIONS

1. What have you been taught about spiritual warfare? Do you find yourself denying or praying against demonic attacks?
2. Are there any areas of your life in which you have given "place" to the devil or allowed your child to do so? What step can you take today to see a change in this area?
3. Read Psalm 91. List the promises of God for you and your household.
4. What is a major lie of the Enemy that you have believed or still believe? Find a Scripture that contradicts the lie and reminds you of God's love for you.

POWER PRAYER

Lord, I come to You asking for protection of my mind, heart, and physical body. I ask this not only for myself but for _____. I am aware that there is a real enemy who desires to kill, steal from, and destroy God's people. Lord, I thank You that at Your name angels can be dispatched, demons must go, and lives can be set free from every form of oppression.

Lord, open my eyes to see any area where I have given place to the Enemy in my own life or _____'s life. Father, I repent for doing so and ask that You give me discernment to know what is right and what must go. Help me to renew my mind daily so that my thoughts, beliefs, and actions line up with Your Word. God, I ask that You help me to accept my identity as Your child and to believe all that You have said over me. If at any time I have allowed the Enemy's voice to ring louder than yours, bring Your correction and help me to walk in Your truth. Lord, I ask that You teach me how to train _____ to know Your voice. Help _____'s identity to be firmly rooted in Your Word so that _____ may reject every lie of the Enemy now and forever. In Jesus's name. Amen.

Chapter Eight

STRATEGIC PRAYER

What a comfort it was for me to know that no matter
where I was in the world, my mother was praying for me.
BILLY GRAHAM

MOTHERS, WE MUST PRAY.

When we're hurting, we must pray.

When life is fabulous, we must pray.

When our children aren't well, we must pray.

When our children are in perfect health, we must pray.

Before we sign our children up for another activity, we must pray.

Before we start or end a job, we must pray.

When we are choosing a church home, we'd better pray!

Before we sign that lease, contract, mortgage, or deal, we must stop and pray.

Many mothers desire to see God move in their families but forget to speak to Him about them. I, too, have even been guilty of running to Google, friends, or my pastor more than God! Many times prayer has become my emergency exit rather than my place of shelter. But if we want to see our spiritual health, mental health, and parenting transformed, we must run to God above all. I have found over and over again that when we run to other things, the fix will only be temporary. In many cases, the anxiety attached to trying to figure something out causes more stress than we can bear. Sadly, some of our deepest anguishes are self-inflicted as we torture ourselves with endless internet searches on how to change our situation. When we seek the world's knowledge more than God's, our situations rarely end well. In 1 Corinthians, Paul wrote, "For the wisdom of this world is foolishness in God's sight. As it is written: 'He catches the wise in their craftiness'; and again, 'The Lord knows that the thoughts of the wise are futile'" (1 Corinthians 3:19–20).

In this battle for our children's spiritual gains, prayer must be the foundation of every move we make. We must run to God more than we run to anything or anyone else. A Christian without prayer is like a soldier without battle gear—defenseless. We're defeated before the war even begins.

One reason the Enemy is wreaking havoc in the lives of many Christians is because they fail to have a relationship with the One they claim to follow. Let me say that again: One reason the Enemy is wreaking havoc is because many "Christians" have no relationship with Christ. This shouldn't be so. It would be much like a soldier getting ready for war and never speaking to his or her commander. It simply wouldn't happen. Can you imagine a soldier running aimlessly into a battle, unsure of where the Enemy was, what weapons to use, or the strategy? It would certainly end in death for him. Warrior Mother, our communication with God can be the difference between life and death. Victory or defeat. Depression or joy. Anxiety or peace. Heaven or hell. We do ourselves and our children a disservice when we fail to ever speak to the Lord but expect Him to rescue us from every situation.

God is our commander. David described this perfectly in Psalms: "Praise the LORD, who is my rock. He trains my hands for war and gives my fingers skill for battle" (Psalm 144:1 NLT).

David was completely aware that he needed God to train him for the battles ahead. He had learned this lesson as a child firsthand when he fought Goliath and experienced it throughout his adulthood as he faced various foes. In life we must accept this perspective that David had if we want to see God move radically in our lives and in our children's. Let our heart cry today be this: "Lord, train my hands for war!" Whereas the world wars with physical weapons, remember, we fight differently. Our powerful prayer is what shakes foundations, breaks chains, and sends the devil fleeing. The time has come for mothers to fight in prayer. We can no longer allow Satan to get the victory in our homes. We must pray for strategy, instruction, clarity, discernment, and wisdom every opportunity we get. When we fail to be women of prayer, we leave our children and ourselves unprotected and vulnerable to attack. Bottom line—prayer is the key to victorious parenting.

A Deeper Dive into Prayer

One of the most interesting requests I've found in the New Testament is asked in Luke 11:1: "One day Jesus was praying in a certain place. When he finished, one of his disciples said to him, 'Lord, teach us to pray, just as John taught his disciples.'" After observing Jesus pray, the disciples desired the same wisdom for themselves. They could have said, "Lord, teach us how You turned water into wine" or "Lord, teach us how to calm a storm with words." Instead, they wanted to know this foundational aspect of how to pray to the Father in heaven. By the time Luke 11 occurs, the men had witnessed Jesus pulling away and publicly praying several times (Matthew 14:23; Luke 3:21; 9:16). Before Jesus multiplied the loaves and fish to feed the multitude, He prayed. Before He called out whom His disciples would be, He prayed. Luke 5:16 says, "Jesus Himself would often slip away to the wilderness and pray" (NASB).

I can imagine the disciples had many moments when they had no idea where Jesus was *only* to find He had left the crowd to pray—again. The disciples took notice of this and wanted to know how they could have an intimate relationship with God for themselves. In other words, *If Jesus does it, I want to do it too.* Jesus was never too busy or tired to pray to the Lord. He made prayer a priority.

I believe there are four key aspects of prayer that we must incorporate to see our homes shift.

Honor

> [Jesus] said to them, "When you pray, say:
> 'Father,
> hallowed be your name,
> your kingdom come.
> Give us each day our daily bread.
> Forgive us our sins,
>   for we also forgive everyone who sins against us.
> And lead us not into temptation.'" (Luke 11:2–4)

One of the first things Jesus did in the prayer He modeled in Luke 11 was teach the disciples that they must honor the Lord. The word *hallowed* here means "holy and set apart." Jesus wanted to set the foundation up front that God is to be recognized for who He is. He is holy, not like us, and worthy to be placed above any and every request. Before we speak a word of prayer or dare ask a thing of God, we must first come to Him with a reverent fear, knowing that He knows all and is the ultimate authority.

As mothers, we cannot glance past this aspect of honor when it comes to prayer. Sadly, many enter prayer with a sense of entitlement. They believe that God owes them and that He'd better move on their behalf. This is a dangerous attitude that implies that God works for us and not that we *live* for Him. Although there certainly are promises that come with being a child of God, we must never forget that God is not our personal genie waiting to answer our every desire. If we don't squash this thought, we will pass down this backward way of thinking to our children. When things go wrong, they will either see it as

- they're not really one of God's children;
- God doesn't care about them; or
- God is not good.

A true picture of Christianity is one in which we honor God above all else. It is one in which we live as a sacrifice unto Him. Every prayer we pray should be filtered through the lens that we serve a BIG God. He is the Creator of heaven and the earth, knows all things, and cannot be ruled by anyone. He always was and always is. He can do what He chooses when He chooses (Psalm 115:3).

Let us not become so conceited to think God owes us anything. His death and resurrection are enough to carry us from now until all eternity. All that He chooses to do for us is out of His great love and infinite wisdom. My prayer is that we never take that for granted. Let us see prayer as a holy moment in which we have the privilege of approaching a God who has more knowledge and power than we could ever imagine. When we go into prayer from a place of humility, our ears will readily submit to all that God has to say to us concerning the matter at hand. The Bible makes it clear that we serve a God who is indescribable. What an honor and privilege to pray to the God who created all things. "For in him all things were created: things in heaven and on earth, visible and invisible, whether thrones or powers or rulers or authorities; all things have been created through him and for him" (Colossians 1:16).

Persist
Knock and keep on knocking.

In Luke 11:9, right after Jesus shared with the disciples how to pray, He shared the importance of persistent prayer. It's okay to pray about a matter more than once. In fact, in most scenarios you should pray multiple times. Although there are differences of opinion about whether you should pray for something once and leave it alone or pray until God moves, this passage makes it clear that God is not offended by your choice to pray about it again.

> Then Jesus said to them, "Suppose you have a friend, and you go to him at midnight and say, 'Friend, lend me three loaves of bread; a friend of mine on a journey has come to me, and I have no food to offer him.' And suppose the one inside answers, 'Don't bother me. The door is already locked,

and my children and I are in bed. I can't get up and give you anything.' I tell you, even though he will not get up and give you the bread because of friendship, yet because of your shameless audacity he will surely get up and give you as much as you need.

"So I say to you: Ask and it will be given to you; seek and you will find; knock and the door will be opened to you. For everyone who asks receives; the one who seeks finds; and to the one who knocks, the door will be opened." (Luke 11:5–10)

Yet our current society has primed us to want quick solutions. We can get frustrated when we pray and don't see immediate answers. Although we may pray about a situation once or twice, we tend to seek alternative solutions or try to fix it ourselves when things don't work out immediately. Jesus tells us in Luke 11:5–10 that God is not annoyed by and does not look down upon persistence. When we ask God for what we need, He will respond.

I experienced this directly while believing for healing for my daughter's epilepsy. According to her neurologist at the time, if a patient goes two years seizure-free, it can be assumed he or she has outgrown the condition. Thankfully, two years passed with my daughter having no seizures. I will never forget how much I prayed leading up to her two-year follow-up appointment from the last seizure. I couldn't help but believe God had healed her and that every scan would show it. After all, I had taken her to several church events where people had prayed over her, and I prayed over her every chance I could. I desperately wanted her to live a life where she wasn't fearful or embarrassed about when the next seizure could happen.

Sadly, I left the two-year appointment disappointed. Not only was she not cleared to stop her medication, but her brain scans were worse. Every six months for the next six years, we would go to the appointment only to be let down again. All the while I continued to pray every chance I could, "Lord, please completely heal my daughter." I am so thankful to say that after ten years of believing for the Lord to do it, He finally did. It took ten years for the manifestation of the prayers I had been praying to come to pass—when the doctor said, "Your daughter is fine and free to stop all seizure medications." Though I couldn't see the victory right away, I chose to stay persistent in prayer even when I was uncertain of the outcome.

A mother without prayer is like a soldier going into war without armor.

God is calling us to persist in prayer for our children. We cannot neglect to cover them with prayer. Daily I hear stories of mothers who have given up on prayer and choose to simply let things happen. Know that if you ever reach a point in any situation where you've decided never to pray about it again, this is not what God would have you do. If it's burdening your heart, God would rather you bare your heart to Him than be silently tormented. First Thessalonians 5:17 (NASB) says, "Pray without ceasing." So rather than being content with the diagnosis, bring your request to God again. It's possible the diagnosis won't change, but perhaps your heart will. Maybe your strategy on how to see your child live a whole life, despite their illness, will start to crystallize. Perhaps God will speak to you tremendously through it.

Again, a mother without prayer is like a soldier going into war without armor. Let us not give the Enemy that advantage. When in doubt, fear, anguish, or irritation, pray about it. And when you're done, pray about it again. In persistent prayer we will find the peace we need. This alone is a victory we cannot overlook. "Do not be anxious about anything, but in every situation, by prayer and petition, with thanksgiving, present your requests to God. And the peace of God, which transcends all understanding, will guard your hearts and your minds in Christ Jesus" (Philippians 4:6–7).

Align with God's Word

Our prayers should not just be honorable or persistent—they should also align with God's Word. I would go as far as to say that when we pray things that contradict biblical truth, it could be seen as witchcraft. If you are praying for someone to be in pain, cursed, or something else sinful, I can assure you that God will not send angels to assist you. You can be certain of this—God will not bless your prayer to marry another person's husband! Nor will He answer your prayer to bring revenge on a certain family member. These are perfect examples of praying against the will of God. Remember, the Bible says the effective, fervent prayer of the *righteous* avails much (James 5:16)! In other words, those who pray strategically and often, with the right motivation, will accomplish much through prayer. If you've been praying from a place of envy, malice, greed, revenge, or condemnation, pause and repent.

When it comes to praying for our children, we can lean into the truth of God's promises. In the Bible you will find countless truths about what God thinks about you and your children. His promises are true and reflect His heart for us. We can believe for health, provision, wisdom, and protection over our children because these things all align with God's promises. Here I'll show you with three scenarios how one can use God's Word as the foundation for powerful prayer.

> **Scenario One**—A mother feels anxious whenever her child isn't close by.
> Biblical passage—"The LORD himself goes before you and will be with you; he will never leave you nor forsake you. Do not be afraid; do not be discouraged" (Deuteronomy 31:8).
> The promise—The Lord promises never to leave us or forsake us.
> The prayer—"Father, I thank You that You never leave my child. Whether at school, home, or church, You never have Your eyes away from us. Lord, I thank You for easing my anxiety. I praise You for loving my children more than I ever could and keeping them near, even when I am far. When I feel

overwhelmed, remind me that You're always close. Send the comfort I need on these days Lord."

Scenario Two—A mother feels that her past disqualifies her from being a good mother.

Biblical passage—"If anyone is in Christ, the new creation has come: The old has gone, the new is here!" (2 Corinthians 5:17).

The promise—God makes all things new.

The prayer—"Lord, I thank You that You have made me new. I praise You for a life that is free from the bondage of sin. Lord, heal the trauma of my past and teach me how to use it for Your glory. I ask that You bless my journey as a mother and remind me that in my weakness, You are strong. I praise You that Your love and grace qualify me to parent well. God, use my past pain to give me a tender heart for my children when they are struggling."

Scenario Three—A mother is struggling financially.

Biblical passage—"I was young and now I am old, yet I have never seen the righteous forsaken or their children begging bread" (Psalm 37:25).

The promise—God takes care of His children.

The prayer—"Father, I believe Your Word. Never have the righteous been forsaken. Lord, I pray for wisdom on how to bring finances into my home. I pray for increase in every area of my life. Lord, I pray that You would send people from the north, south, east, and west to ease this burden. God, I know all resources belong to You. Your riches are unimaginable. I thank You that You have not forgotten us and that You will use this time as a part of my testimony. I receive every blessing You have for me and my family. Lord, show me Your goodness in this season so that I can care for my home."

These are just three of an estimated four thousand promises in God's Word. I assure you that there is a promise for every situation. Let us be bold enough to pray in accordance with His will and His Word. Doing so will build your faith. And here's the great news—God's Word never fails. When we pray His words over us, these prayers will always lead us to victory. Every time we pray from a place of recognizing His promises, we can do so boldly. We can do so because the Word reminds us that God remains true and cannot lie. "God is not human, that he should lie, not a human being, that he should change his mind. Does he speak and then not act? Does he promise and not fulfill?" (Numbers 23:19).

Open Your Ears

Every time we come to God, we should do so with our hearts and ears open. Prayer isn't just about bringing our requests and pain. It is also about listening for God's response. So often we moms come to God with petitions—for example, to ask Him to take away our child's ailments or give us strength to endure the pressures of parenting. However, when we pray, we must be just as open to listening as we are to speak. I appreciate the old saying "God gave you two ears and one mouth so you can listen more than you talk." Although we may not hear God in an audible voice all around us, He certainly communicates to us in many ways. Whether it be that still, small voice that tells us to pause or a child sharing his or her heart on a matter, He speaks. He speaks through worship music. He speaks through nature and even in calamity. Our job is not to be too busy, anxious, or convinced we know the answer that we forget to listen.

Recently I found myself feeling like I must pray for my children's health immediately. Although no one was physically ill, I just couldn't fight the overwhelming sensation that I needed to pray. As usual, I prayed that God would cover them from the top of their heads to the bottom of their feet. I prayed for their organs, limbs, minds, and emotions to function in complete health. And when I was finished praying for every little part of them, I just sat quietly.

It was then that I heard the voice of the Lord whisper to my heart, "What are you doing to help them be healthy?" Ouch! In that moment, the Lord brought a well-needed correction. I had been pacifying my children with candy to get them to behave. My schedule was so frantic and busy that relying on fast food was easier than a home-cooked meal. Even for their mental health, my lack of organization left them unsure of whether we were coming or going. So, yes, although I was praying for their health to be whole, I certainly wasn't doing much to help! From that moment forward, I committed to seeking God for how I can help my children be well from the inside out.

In other words, it's not enough just to pray. You must be willing to listen and hear what the Lord has to say. He holds infinite wisdom and happens to be the Creator of the very children you're praying for. Could it be that He knows exactly what they need or don't need? Remember, prayer is about a dialogue between you and the Lord, not a monologue of your requests. God is looking for mothers who will rise up and respond to His voice. This is how you will see the blessings of God overflow in your home. May your prayer be this: "Lord, give me ears to hear what Your Spirit is speaking." Be fully committed to where He leads, and watch how your life will change. "For the eyes of the LORD range throughout the earth to strengthen those whose hearts are fully committed to him" (2 Chronicles 16:9).

Seeking God for Your Child

Intercession is a key aspect of prayer. To intercede means to take another person's place or to plead on their behalf. When we pray for our children who may be too young or don't have a relationship with Jesus, we are pleading on their behalf. When we do so, we are saying, "God, I stand in the place of my children and believe for _____."
Even Jesus and Paul prayed for those they were called to disciple. In fact, almost every letter of Paul starts and ends with a prayer. He was serious about seeking God for those He had been called to minister to, and Jesus did the same with His disciples. Let's take a moment to look at a powerful prayer spoken by Jesus. I encourage you to pull out

a pen or highlighter and take note of all the many ways this prayer should mirror a mother's heart.

> I have revealed you to those whom you gave me out of the world. They were yours; you gave them to me and they have obeyed your word. Now they know that everything you have given me comes from you. For I gave them the words you gave me and they accepted them. They knew with certainty that I came from you, and they believed that you sent me. I pray for them. I am not praying for the world, but for those you have given me, for they are yours. All I have is yours, and all you have is mine. And glory has come to me through them. I will remain in the world no longer, but they are still in the world, and I am coming to you. Holy Father, protect them by the power of your name, the name you gave me, so that they may be one as we are one. While I was with them, I protected them and kept them safe by that name you gave me. None has been lost except the one doomed to destruction so that Scripture would be fulfilled.
>
> I am coming to you now, but I say these things while I am still in the world, so that they may have the full measure of my joy within them. I have given them your word and the world has hated them, for they are not of the world any more than I am of the world. My prayer is not that you take them out of the world but that you protect them from the evil one. They are not of the world, even as I am not of it. Sanctify them by the truth; your word is truth. As you sent me into the world, I have sent them into the world. For them I sanctify myself, that they too may be truly sanctified. (John 17:6–19)

There are a few aspects of this prayer of intercession we should lean into.

- Jesus recognized that the disciples were not His own (verses 6–10). Considering this, we must come to God knowing we are praying for His children. This reminds us to be humble and remember that He knows best. It also releases some of the burden to feel like we need to have all the answers or solve all their issues.
- He prayed for their protection (verses 11–12). As mothers, we should be praying daily for our children's safety. Never hesitate to pray for God to keep them shielded from every attack of the Enemy. From accidents to sickness, to abuse of any sort, keep your children covered. Pray that the Holy Spirit would warn them of danger and that angels would be dispatched to guard them against all harm.
- He prayed for them to be clean (verses 17–18). Jesus prayed that the disciples would be sanctified through truth. What a powerful prayer! As we intercede for our children, we need to pray that they encounter the truth and that they not become confused by the ways of this world. Let us cry out that they stay holy and grounded in truth no matter what lies the Enemy tries to bring about. These prayers can be lifted before you see a hint of a poor life choice, during a trying time, or even after they have been set free from bondages.
- He recognized His part in their lives (verses 8, 12, 14, 19). During this prayer of intercession, Jesus took ownership of how He had helped the disciples draw closer to the Father. He said in essence, "I have taught them Your Word. I have protected them. I have kept them safe, and I have sanctified myself for their sakes." In other words, a part of intercession is recognizing what God is calling you to do beyond your prayer. Are you willing to act on what God speaks to you in prayer? As we pray for our children, we need also to recognize that the entire responsibility doesn't just fall on God. He has called us to do His will on earth. Jesus reminds us to both pray and act.

Fasting to Hear from God More Clearly

Fasting is another aspect of prayer that seems to go neglected in modern Christianity. To fast means to abstain from something desired, particularly food. The Bible provides several examples of fasting leading to answered prayer, clarity for the battle ahead, and victory. Moses fasted before receiving the Ten Commandments. Esther asked the Jews to fast alongside her before she approached the king about saving her people from genocide. Jesus fasted for forty days and nights directly after His baptism. And while the believers were fasting in Acts, the Holy Spirit directed them to send out Paul and Barnabas for the work of the ministry. Moments of transition, temptation, or frustration can be managed with greater ease when we join prayer with fasting. One of the most astonishing outcomes from fasting is recorded in Mark 9:25–29 (NKJV):

> When Jesus saw that the people came running together, He rebuked the unclean spirit, saying to it, "Deaf and dumb spirit, I command you, come out of him and enter him no more!" Then the spirit cried out, convulsed him greatly, and came out of him. And he became as one dead, so that many said, "He is dead." But Jesus took him by the hand and lifted him up, and he arose.
>
> And when He had come into the house, His disciples asked Him privately, "Why could we not cast it out?"
>
> So He said to them, "This kind can come out by nothing but prayer and fasting."

Jesus made a clear distinction here that some trials require a time of prayer *and* fasting. Some situations aren't going to change without you taking a moment to get steady and clear out any distraction that is blocking you from hearing the Lord. A true biblical fast involves abstaining from food. For Daniel, it was not eating meat. Jesus fasted all food. In today's time, we may see a variation in how we fast or what we choose to fast from. Some will fast from sweets, others a certain meal of the day, and others will attempt to completely fast from food. Others may find that what's distracting them is time watching television or consuming social media. When entering a fast, pray about what, how long, and why you are doing so. We don't fast for fun or for people to notice but to hear God's voice. Let's be clear—we aren't fasting to lose weight or to kick-start our diet at the beginning of the year. While there's nothing wrong with getting healthy, the focus of spiritual fasts is God, not ourselves.

I encourage you to pause and fast before your next big decision. We can fall into such a routine of making quick decisions and praying emergency prayers that we forget to slow down and really hear God. What would it look like for you to intentionally deny yourself something you enjoy *just* to hear from God? We aren't fasting to get things from God or manipulate Him into doing what we want Him to do. If you start off your fasting journey with the concept of "God, I am fasting so I can see You do _____ or fix _____," you are already on the wrong track. Instead, "I am fasting because I want to hear Your voice in my children's lives." "I am fasting because my home is unsettled and I am believing for strategy." "I am fasting because I feel like my life is so busy, I can't hear You." "I am fasting because I know that with prayer and fasting things change." "I am fasting because I surrender it all to You."

What if mothers said with conviction down in their souls, *I am willing to do anything (but sin) to hear God's voice!* This is the heart of a warrior. This is relentless faith and commitment to see you and your child's life changed. "Lord, if You are calling me to put down that chocolate, deactivate my social media, or only drink juice to hear You, I'm here for it. I want to hear You and walk in Your will by any means necessary."

Generational Influence

One area that must be addressed when praying for our children is recognizing the impact of generational influence. It is possible that there are some behaviors, attitudes, and predispositions that our children walked into just by the nature of their last name. In modern Christianity, there is much debate about if the generational curses you see mentioned in the Old Testament ended with Jesus or if they continue to this day. Rather than argue this, I want to speak to you more about the impact our great-great-grandparents may be having on us even today. Being aware of what you may have carried into your parenting should not be a source of shame but rather empowerment.

We can look at the Bible and see how choices made by some impact us even now. The sinful nature that began when Adam took that forbidden bite in the garden has not left us to this day. We are still inherently sinful creatures. In the same way, women still endure pain in childbirth, just as God said, due to Eve's sin. The sin of two people has had a ripple effect for countless generations.

But I also want to encourage you with people like Abraham, whose blessing in Genesis has carried down to us now. Let us not forget that one person's blameless life has also meant freedom for us. With that said, as we look into the lives of those who have come and gone before us, let us not be fooled into thinking it's all bad. The idea is that the Lord will enlighten us to see areas where we've allowed the same patterns to creep into our homes.

As a professor of developmental and social psychology who's also certified in marriage and family therapy, I can say that without a doubt, the secular world is very aware of the impact of the generations before us. This is why a counseling session always begins with a complete overview of the family background. The therapist wants to know who's who, who's still married, who was an addict, and so on. The therapist knows before she even gets to your issues that she first has to take inventory of the people who aren't in the room. Even your medical doctor won't start work on you until they know your family history. I find that only Christians shy away from the idea that some things Grandma may have struggled with fifty years ago may be affecting your children now. Here's the thing: the devil is not the new kid in the school of life—you are. He's been around long enough that he knows exactly what your family's weaknesses are. In the Bible, these demonic spirits that attach to families and attempt to destroy them are called familiar spirits (Leviticus 19:31; Isaiah 8:9).

Here's what I know: at the name of Jesus, He can break every curse that may be attached to your name. Those bondages, addictions, and wicked lifestyles can end right now with you recognizing them, calling them out, and praying against them. Dr. Lance Wallnau speaks of the power of generational influence:

> If the pattern has been evident in your bloodline, perhaps you are the one who gets the task of finally breaking it off of your household and the next generation! This is where you become the champion that cuts off the pattern of iniquity or the power of a familiar spirit from operating because you choose to resist it and break the cycle in your own life. That's really what an overcomer is.[1]

Over the next few days or weeks, learn everything you can about your family. The more generations you can go back, the better. If you don't have access to your biological parents, grandparents, or cousins, that's okay. For this part, just go with what you know, and pray. God can reveal things about your family in prayer *and* fasting that you might never have known. In my own life, I have uncovered patterns of addiction, divorce, cancer, anxiety, and more. As you learn information, I encourage you to create an Awareness Tree (see example on the next page) and use the labels listed to pick up patterns that may be present. As you write out each person's name or title (e.g., paternal grandmother), also notate with initials any addictions, poverty, early death, divorce, or sin, as listed in the key below. In the center circle labeled "Me," list all you have dealt with. Again, this is not to cause shame but to shed light on the Enemy's devices. You can't pray against something you aren't aware of. If you have access to this information about the father of your children, do the same! You will instantly start to see patterns.

Sample Awareness Tree

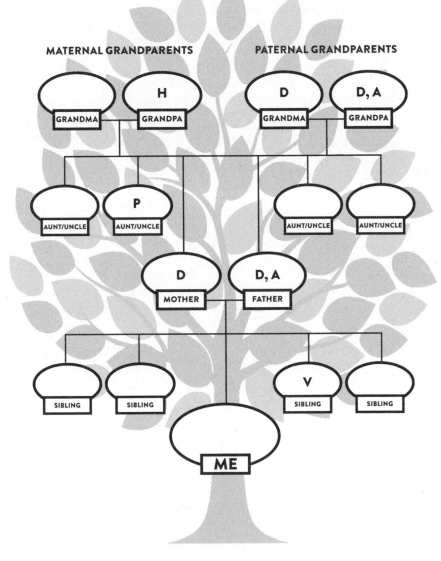

MATERNAL GRANDPARENTS   **PATERNAL GRANDPARENTS**

| GRANDMA | H GRANDPA | D GRANDMA | D, A GRANDPA |

| AUNT/UNCLE | P AUNT/UNCLE | AUNT/UNCLE | AUNT/UNCLE |

| D MOTHER | D, A FATHER |

| SIBLING | SIBLING | V SIBLING | SIBLING |

ME

Awareness Key

- **A**—addiction
- **D**—divorce
- **S**—sexual sin: fornication, adultery, homosexuality
- **P**—poverty
- **E**—early death, unusual accidents that ended in death
- **F**—extreme fear, paranoia, or panic attacks
- **M**—mental health disorders, depression, schizophrenia, bipolar
- **H**—health crises: cancer, terminal illness, rare disorders or diseases, heart disease
- **V**—violent natured, hatefulness, abusive
- **W**—witchcraft

Take Authority

Warrior Mother, I want to say this from the depths of my soul. By the power of the name of Jesus Christ, you have been given authority! Far too often we shrink back and allow the devil to run rampant in our families. When trials come, we retreat rather than fighting in prayer and standing on God's Word. We've allowed the attacks of the Enemy to rob us of our sanity, to lead our children into sinful lifestyles, and to leave us in despair. I say, "No more." Your soul should say, "Never again." This authority that you have as a believer is not because you're so great or powerful. This dominion you carry is because the same power and Spirit that raised Christ from the dead dwells within you (Romans 8:11). Let's turn to the Word on this topic.

- "When Jesus had called the Twelve together, he gave them power and authority to drive out all demons and to cure diseases" (Luke 9:1).
- "I have given you authority to trample on snakes and scorpions and to overcome all the power of the Enemy; nothing will harm you" (Luke 10:19).

- "Then Jesus came to them and said, 'All authority in heaven and on earth has been given to me'" (Matthew 28:18).
- "Truly I tell you, whatever you bind on earth will be bound in heaven, and whatever you loose on earth will be loosed in heaven" (Matthew 18:18).

My prayer is that seeing those generational patterns ignited something within you to fight for your children. We don't have to settle any longer. Remember, a warrior is *actively* involved in warfare. I've heard people say things like, "Everyone in my family has heart issues, so I probably will too" and "The men in my family cheat—we just can't help it." In so many ways, we can allow the sins of our fathers and mothers to become our own. Warrior Mother, rather than sit back and say, "Well, my family just struggles with this. This is how its always been, so it's how it's just going to be," we have to break off this mindset and say, "This ends here."

The truth is, you don't need to create a long prayer and gather the top leaders of your church to pray against patterns of disease, sin, or addiction in your family tree. Instead, you can simply stand in authority and pray, "In the name of Jesus, we pray against _____ that has troubled those in the generations before. I break every agreement with _____ and ask for wisdom on how to avoid walking into the same traps as those who have come before me. This sin of _____ ends with me, and I proclaim victory over it for myself and my future generations. In Jesus's name!"

There is no magic formula—only believers standing in authority and proclaiming God's Word over our situation. Remember, we are not victims of circumstance and can declare His truth over every circumstance in expectation that He will fight every demon, generational influence, and spiritual battle that attempts to destroy us. Stand on the Word of God and pray those demons and generational strongholds off you and your family. Your prayers are powerful!

Our children don't have to be helpless casualties of spritual warfare because we neglected to pray. Before we seek to transform our homes, we must first transform our hearts toward prayer. God is always speaking—may we never be too busy to slow down and listen.

Pray.

Listen.

Believe.

Act.

──────────────── VICTORY VERSE ────────────────

Devote yourselves to prayer, being watchful and thankful. (Colossians 4:2)

──────────────── REFLECTIONS ────────────────

1. How much has prayer been a priority for you and your family?
2. Which of the following is your strength when it comes to prayer: honor, persistence, aligning with God's Word, having open ears, or fasting? Is there an area you feel the Holy Spirit is leading you to focus on?
3. When it comes to generational influence, list some positive factors of your family's past that you can see within yourself and your child (examples: resilience, strength, compassion).
4. List five things you need to commit to prayer about today, and consider fasting for clarity on the matter at hand.

──────────────── POWER PRAYER ────────────────

Dear heavenly Father, I thank You for who You are. I give You all the praise and glory for being a part of my story. God, I come to You humbly, knowing that You choose to love me despite my shortcomings. Forgive me if I have neglected our relationship. Lord, I need You more than ever to show up in my life and in the lives of those You have entrusted me with. God, my heart is open to Your will and Your way for my family. Teach me to hear You; teach me to follow; teach me to believe what You say. Correct me when I allow pride to convince me that I know better than You. Give me an open heart to receive and a strategy to know how to act on Your Word. Lord, I pray against every generational influence that may be causing _____ to fall into sin. I call out the following sinful natures and predispositions and declare that they cannot have dominion in my home.

In the name of Jesus, I rebuke the spirit of addiction and say, "Go!" May every desire to compulsively run to a substance or any idol be taken away from me and my children.

I pray against all perverseness in my bloodline—sexual addictions, fornication, lustful spirits, pornography addiction, pedophilia, homosexual desires, and anything that goes against God's original intent for sex. Show me how to overcome these moments of weakness by walking in Your Spirit.

May generational sicknesses such as cancer, heart disease, sickle cell, epilepsy, diabetes, depression, and anxiety no longer have a stronghold. I pray against the spirit of infirmity over _____'s health. I pray they walk in the healing provided by You. May their story defy any diagnosis given to them.

In Jesus's name, I pray against the spirit of death. I pray long life over each child. I pray against accidental death, premature death, suicidal thoughts, and any other attack that would attempt to rob my family of their lives.

May every familiar spirit that seeks to destroy me and my children go now in the name of Jesus. Familiar spirit, You have no authority over my house, our hearts, our mental health, and our physical health. We pray that the blood of Jesus covers us *now* in Jesus's name! Lord, I repent for any words I've used to come into agreement with these ailments of the heart and mind. Father, give me strategy to break free from any of these things that still have a stronghold in my life. I plead on behalf of my children and grandchildren (now and in the future) that every curse attached to our bloodline be abolished. Give us eyes to see when the Enemy is at work, and restore what has been lost. In Jesus's name. Amen!

Once you've prayed today's prayer, do whatever you have to do to see your family set free. Throw away anything (magazines, movies, books, alcohol, etc.) that may be a stumbling block and give Satan a foothold in your life. Make a choice to let your prayers not be in vain, and break the power of the Enemy in your and your child's life.

Chapter Nine

MODELING THE FAITH

Once established, reputations do not easily change.
ALBERT BANDURA

YOU'RE JUST LIKE YOUR MOTHER!

For some reason, in our society, this phrase has become a dreaded thing to hear. So many spend a lifetime trying to outrun the traits, mannerisms, and sayings of their mothers. But the older we get, the more our upbringing seeps into our everyday reality. So much so that studies have concluded that biological traits tend to become more prevalent the older a person gets.[1] In other words, the older you are, the more likely you are to respond, think, and act like your parents. Chances are, if I meet you, I will see some traits of your family seeping through. Perhaps the curl of your lip when you smile, your inflection when you're angry, or the way you walk looks a lot like your biological mother, even if you've never interacted with her.

Luckily, growing up to be like my mother wouldn't be the worst thing to happen to me. My mother was a sweetheart (if I kept my room clean and behaved well in public). I recognize that I am one of the fortunate ones and that for some people, growing up to reflect their parents is a legitimate fear. Yet as we discussed in the previous chapter, having traits of those before you can be a blessing. Your mother may have been known for her resilience, being a diligent worker, or having the best recipes in town. Or even better, your family may be known for their faith or their heart for other people.

My favorite biblical passage on this matter is in Paul's second letter to Timothy. Timothy was a young minister of the gospel who needed some encouragement as he started to lead churches. Rather than tell Timothy how he would likely fail or that he needed to just get it together, Paul inspired him with these words: "I am reminded of your sincere faith, which first lived in your grandmother Lois and in your mother Eunice and, I am persuaded, now lives in you also. For this reason I remind you to fan into flame the gift of God, which is in you through the laying on of my hands" (2 Timothy 1:5–6).

In this passage, Timothy was reminded that he was not the first person of great faith in his family. His mother and his grandmother lived in sincere faith and trusted God. And for that reason, Paul could confidently say to Timothy in so many words, "Hey, kid, I know you have what it takes to do this. Your mother had it. Your grandmother gave it to her, and now you have it. So walk in it!" In this passage, Paul was calling out the fact that Timothy grew up in an environment that reflected the Christian walk. Timothy's mission to lead churches was simply the next step of walking in the gifts that were fostered in his upbringing. Timothy's lineage had provided a foundation for him to model. This is what we are called to do as well.

God desires for mothers to truly commit to modeling the faith. The great news is that you are not bound by the traits or dysfunction of your parents. You can parent uniquely the way God has called you to do. The key is to parent from a place where you are a genuine example of Christlike character. Playing church on Sunday or expecting the local children's ministry to instruct your kids about Jesus will simply not do. Building Christian character starts at home. All other influences, whether they be the private school up the street, the youth group, or the Christian college, are merely supplements to what you are already doing. We see in the Old Testament that teaching your children about God was not a suggestion. "These commandments that I give you today are to be on your hearts. Impress them on your children. Talk about them when you sit at home and when you walk along the road, when you lie down and when you get up. Tie them as symbols on your hands and bind them on your foreheads. Write them on the doorframes of your houses and on your gates" (Deuteronomy 6:6–9).

Consider how Jesus reacted when he noticed His disciples shooing away children who were hungry to learn from Him: "When Jesus saw this, he was indignant. He said to them, 'Let the little children come to me, and do not hinder them, for the kingdom of God belongs to such as these. Truly I tell you, anyone who will not receive the kingdom of God like a little child will never enter it.'" (Mark 10:14–15).

Jesus loved children and wanted them to hear the gospel as well. We should never find ourselves depending solely on another person or organization to share God with our children. Surely the Lord won't be looking to the local pastor to give an account for how *you* raised your child; He will be looking to you. I am convinced that sharing the Bible is only the beginning of modeling the faith. If we truly want to show our children what it looks like to have a relationship with God, we must first recognize how our actions may be impacting them. The Great Commission starts at home. If we want to win souls and make disciples as the Lord has commanded, we had better start with examining ourselves.

Observation Matters

When it comes to learning, observation is the cornerstone. It is believed that 65 percent of all learners are visual and 35 percent are auditory.[2] This means that most people pick up their behavior from what they see modeled before them or what they hear in their environment. Thus, the adage "do what I say and not what I do" is a meaningless phrase. It's most likely that your child will do what they see you do and repeat what they hear you say. Most parents have probably learned this the hard way.

Simply put, observation matters. Our children naturally imitate us. This was brought to my attention years ago with my daughter Trinity. At the time, she was two years old. I noticed that every time she got frustrated, she would say "Oh my God" under her breath. My first thought was, *Where did she get that from?* Then I realized . . . she got it from me! In fact, how she said it was exactly the way I would say it. Certainly there were worse things she could say. But for many this phrase would be seen as a Christian curse phrase and using the Lord's name in vain. This alone would bring quick judgment from some of my Christian friends if said in public. I explained to her that it's better to say "oh my goodness" or a cuter phrase like "cheese and sprinkles." It took months to break her out of that habit. Admittedly, this was one of the lesser bad phrases I've had to break my children out of.

The power of influence also resonates with adults. In a conversation with Major Garrett Gray of the Army National Guard, I asked, "Who was your favorite leader since serving in the military?" He instantly shared about one of his previous lieutenant colonels who had shown him what true leadership looked like. His previous lieutenant colonel was not in the habit of just barking orders. Instead, he modeled leadership by being timely, stern but truthful, and setting a high standard. Having this lieutenant reminded Major Gray of the heart of what it meant to be a part of the US military and gave him someone to look up to. Major Gray insists that he owes much of his success to the example shown by this superior early in his career. Major Gray provided the perfect example of how one person's actions can change the course of your life.

The phenomenon of the importance of modeling is one that can be backed up spiritually and in everyday life. According to the Word of God, you can expect that how you behave has a tremendous influence. First Corinthians 15:33 reminds us of this when it says, "Bad company corrupts good character." In the same way, Paul addressed Timothy by reminding him that he must set an example for his followers "in speech, in conduct, in love, in faith and in purity" (1 Timothy 4:12). Jesus also had a say in this. He said that anyone who causes one of his children to stumble will face consequences (Matthew 18:6–8). Let's go a step further and recognize that Jesus said that the way people will know you are a Christian is not by how much you attend church or quote Scripture but by how you love (John 13:35). In other words, God is serious about us not just talking about Him but living a lifestyle that reflects Him.

Not surprisingly, much research has brought to life the power of observation. The most famous theorist on social learning was Albert Bandura. According to Bandura, children will model and form opinions on what is moral based on those around them. Even more so, the person who holds the greatest weight as the primary caregiver will set the tone for how a child reacts and responds. In his words, "People not only gain understanding through reflection, they evaluate and alter their own thinking."[3] And so it's not just *what we do* but also *how we respond* to what our children do that sets the foundation for behavior.

Bandura proved this idea in his famous Bobo doll experiment. In this study, children were split into three distinct groups and shown how adults responded to a doll named Bobo. One group observed an adult being extraordinarily aggressive to the doll; the next group witnessed an adult being kind to the doll; the third group had no model that interacted with the doll. Shortly after, the children were left in a room one by one with the Bobo doll. Over and over, researchers observed that children who had witnessed the aggressive behavior (regardless of the child's gender) showed extreme aggression toward the Bobo doll. However, those who had seen the model be gentle interacted with the Bobo doll in a kind and loving manner.[4] This study makes it clear that from only moments of observation, a child can easily decide what is deemed appropriate or inappropriate behavior. Imagine how this phenomenon increases in prevalence with children we interact with daily!

As a mother, I have learned it is much easier to teach life-giving behaviors than to break destructive habits. Sometimes we spend too much time looking to outside sources for explanations for our children's behaviors. *Video games made our children violent. Television shows taught them inappropriate words. The kids at school made ours disrespectful.* Yet when we're least expecting it, our children are observing us much more than we believe! And of course, God is too. He has entrusted us with them. So we must see our influence in their lives as a crucial part of their faith walk.

I want to present you with a harsh truth: kids can spot a hypocrite from a mile away. I cannot count how many times I've heard the phrase, "But you said." In a society where children have access to so many influences, the days of "because I told you so" are long gone. We cannot be angry when our children say something or participate in a sin that we normalize. In fact, you give indirect permission for your child to behave in an unsatisfactory manner every time you contradict yourself in this way. Of course, no parent will be perfect. However, we should actively seek to examine our behavior and ask ourselves, *If my child said or acted like this, how would I feel?* This should pause our actions and cause us to make a change. Let's take a moment to talk about different areas we have to address if we want to see our children grow closer to the Lord.

How You Treat People

As mentioned earlier, the number one way the world will know you are a follower of Christ is by how you love others. Our children are watching how we talk about the people at our workplace. They're seeing how we respond to the cashier when the total isn't what we expected. For those who are married, our children are watching how we respond to our husbands. Are we rude? Do we disrespect him in private or call him our "other child"? What about our children? Do we respond with love when aggravated? Are our words hurtful, abusive, uncaring, selfish, demanding, or tainted by our annoyance toward them?

Our children are also observing how we give to others. Certainly they notice when you stop everything to help a friend or pray for a person in need. A fitting example of this is how you respond to a person asking for food or money on a street corner. Do you look down on him in contempt or roll your window up and act like you don't see him? Something as simple as giving a couple of dollars, some food, or a kind word will cause your children to reflect on how they should respond in such scenarios. We set the foundation for how to love people well. In my home I can always tell when it's time to do a self-checkup. When I hear my children bickering incessantly, I can trace it back to how I interacted with them or their father earlier that day. In the same way, they have moments when they are unusually kind and considerate of one another. It seems that these moments are spawned from the times I didn't yell over spilled milk or gave a second chance when a mistake was made. I see on a daily basis that the more I model love, the more they will follow.

How You Respond to Trials

Children observe how we respond in crisis. I've found in my own life that I can be strong on Sunday morning, but when tough times come, I struggle. My typical bubbly self can turn into someone who is stressed, irritable, and overwhelmed when things go wrong. Without a doubt, when I sing to the Lord about my faith at church but wallow in self-pity shortly after, it causes my children to wonder if my Christian walk is genuine. In an ideal world, shouldn't I be just as fired up in faith when things go wrong as I am when things go right? If we want to model our faith, this doesn't happen on accident. We must become so secure in the fact that God loves us and is working all things out for our good that no situation can hinder us.

One way for our children to observe our faith is for us to run to prayer when we are overwhelmed. When we face a trial, our first response should be prayer and not doubt. I cannot count how many times I gathered my family in our living room to pray together for tough situations. I've called on them to pray for me when my migraines were incessant. We prayed as a family when we experienced a government shutdown that left us without pay for over a month. Not only did this bring a sense of unity, but it also gave us all an opportunity to rejoice when God answered the prayer. Our children were able to see in real time that when we seek God, He responds. If we want to show our children how to stand firm in battles, we must do so ourselves. Although we will have hard moments and times of weakness, let's form a habit of being the prayer warriors that our children can run to in their times of need.

How You Talk About the Church

If you attend a local church, be careful how you discuss it in front of your children. Spending time speaking poorly about the pastor, the services offered, or church drama will plant a negative seed within your children. Church is supposed to be a place where people who are broken come together in unity to know Christ better. But the truth is, the church will never be perfect, because it's full of imperfect people. Members will sometimes want things that can't be fulfilled due to staffing, time, or lack of funds. As a church planter alongside my husband, I know this full well. So when we openly share our disdain for the local church, we give our children reason not to want to attend, and we decrease the value it brings to their lives.

Years ago my husband and I attended a church where we experienced immense hurt. So much so that we talked and fought about it daily. One day my eight-year-old son looked at me and said, "Why are we going there if you hate it so much? We don't like to go somewhere that makes our parents sad." Little did I realize how much our frustrations had been observed. Although there was some truth to my son's words, he developed this feeling because of our conversations about and attitudes toward the church. It took years to reverse this idea and to help our children see that the church is a safe place for our family to grow and flourish. Since then, my children have found a love for ministry, serving in children's church, media, and worship. Once I changed my tone about the church, they changed theirs.

How You Worship

Raising your hands during church is a fantastic way to worship. If you're like me and you love to have worship music playing through your home, amazing! We can see countless stories of worship shifting the atmosphere in the Old Testament. Before battles the warriors would sing out their praises with instruments and voices of triumph. As their praises went up, the Lord showed up mightily. I would encourage you to take your worship to the next level. You don't have to be a great singer, but singing songs and rejoicing to music that glorifies God is a sure way to find peace.

As your children observe you lifting your spirits through worship, they may be more likely to run to this same music when tough times come. God still ministers through melody. I would encourage you to lift your hands, clap, dance, or even create a new song to the Lord when excited or in times of frustration. When we praise, God shows up and worry flees.

However, listening to your favorite Christian songs is only one aspect of worship. True worship comes from giving your all and having a surrendered heart. My questions to you are, Does your life reflect the heart of worship? Do you bring your time, talent, and treasure to God without pause? Are you too busy to serve at your local church or where there is a need? Do you use your God-given talents to bless others, or do you tend to keep them to yourself? Are you reluctant to give to a ministry in need or a person in a financial crisis? These all reflect a heart that recognizes that God owns everything and that He is worthy of all our resources.

When the Lord speaks or leads us to do something, our response can be an act of worship. Our children are watching how we live for God and how we give to God. If we are closefisted with our gifts (talent, time, support), we can expect they will model the same. Being able to worship the Lord with all that we have is a privilege. If we find that we are worshipping anything else above God, we are guilty of putting things, people, and dreams above Him. Yes, even good things can be an idol and a distraction to your Christian faith. If you are obsessed with fitness, money, pleasing others, social media, your personal ministry, or even your appearance, your child will take notice.

My prayer for you today is that you would model a lifestyle of worship by constantly ensuring that God is your priority. Having idols is not a small thing to God. In fact, not putting anything else before God is so important that we find it listed as the first commandment given to Moses in the Old Testament. "You must not have any other god but me. You must not make for yourself an idol of any kind or an image of anything in the heavens or on the earth or in the sea" (Exodus 20:3–4). Yes, even from the beginning of time, the Lord knew that people would struggle with making Him a priority. Let us never find ourselves worshipping or giving more attention to anything more than we serve our God.

How You Share the Bible

Recognizing how you share the Bible in your home is also important. It can be quite easy to take this life-giving manual and use it to bring much harm. We see this often in religious cults that claim to be founded on God's truth. In these environments, the Bible is used to establish the leader as the supreme being and to manipulate the members of the cult. Rather than sharing the Word with love, it is shared in a twisted way that leaves many abused, neglected, and hating the Bible altogether. This is why we are taught in 2 Timothy to study the Word so that we can rightly divide, or interpret, it. Many passages, especially in the Old Testament, when taken out of context or without regard for whom the writing addressed, can be highly swayed and cause much harm. If we ever find ourselves twisting Scripture to manipulate or justify our bad behavior, we must repent.

Our sharing of the Bible shouldn't be a weapon but a tool for restoration. When it comes to modeling our faith, we must be certain to take inventory of how God and His Word are being presented. The Bible was presented to me when I was a child as a way out of hell. If you don't lie, steal, or cheat, God may be so kind to let you in the gates. Throughout my childhood, this concept haunted me. By the time I was eighteen, I had prayed the sinner's prayer hundreds of times in hopes of making it to heaven. And although living a holy life and God's demand for righteousness is true, I was never taught about God's love. The Bible was a rule book only and never a love letter. Thus, when I got older and truly accepted Jesus into my heart, I couldn't fathom how the same God who couldn't wait to send me to hell for sneaking an extra cookie could suddenly love me. It took years for me to see the Bible in a different light.

The Bible is meant to encourage, not discourage.

Uplift, not destroy.

Heal, not wound.

Mend, not break,

Elevate, not deflate.

When we are sharing the Word with our children, we must be intentional about using it as an opportunity to uplift them. Here are a few suggestions to make the sharing of your faith relevant and even fun.

- Buy each child a Bible based on his or her reading level.
- Allow the child to choose a devotional. (There are many kinds, from superhero to princess to magazine-style devotionals.)
- When your child is frustrated about a trial, draw him or her back to a biblical character and how he or she overcame a struggle.
- When your children feel unloved or insecure, share Bible verses that reflect God's love for them.
- When they feel down, draw them to the Psalms and how God is our comfort in tough times.
- When they aren't sure what choice to make, lead them to the Proverbs.
- Pray together as a family for difficult situations.
- Lay hands on them and pray for them when they aren't feeling well.
- Pray for them when a big event is about to occur.
- Create a back-and-forth journal in which they share their prayer requests one day and you respond with a prayer the next.
- When you learn about a person who is struggling, pray as a family.

These are just a few suggestions for your family to have the Word as a foundation of your home. Overall, your home should reflect what we find in Joshua 24:15: "But as for me and my household, we will serve the LORD!"

We can instill in our children now that God has all the answers. We can show them that God desires to have a relationship with them. If we model that God is a safe place now, we can have confidence that this will be instilled in their hearts. Now is a wonderful day to start modeling your faith in a practical way. Even if your children stray away as they get older, the Lord promises, "Direct your children onto the right path, and when they are older, they will not leave it" (Proverbs 22:6 NLT).

And if your child isn't under your direct influence at the moment due to distance, age, or having his or her own family, you can still have impact. Many of the above suggestions can easily be applied through text messages, a phone call, or even mailing him or her a devotional or Bible. If your child is far away from God, you can still pray for them, you can still model the faith, and you can still find ways to share the Word. Ask the Lord for witty ideas on how to do so.

Outside Influences

Although we may be the primary influence, we cannot overlook the fact that many other people and things shape our children's worlds. As parents, we must take an examination of who and what we allow to speak into their lives. As we saw in chapter 8, we are to give no place to the Enemy (Ephesians 4:27). What other people directly influence your child? Is there a negative aunt who always talks down about your Christian walk? Does your child's favorite YouTuber happen to be an atheist? Are your children's friends or their parents living a lifestyle that contradicts your Christian faith?

You will not be able to micromanage every interaction. This is especially true if your children go to school (public or private) or if they interact with people . . . ever. There will always be someone who disagrees with the Christian faith, has a different conviction on controversial topics, or doesn't adhere to your standard of living. But guard your child as much as possible. Your children may only be able to spend limited time with some family members because their beliefs or viewing habits are incompatible with your values. You cannot allow yourself to carry guilt over saying no or shifting relationships when you see that they're causing harm.

I want to be clear. As Christians, yes, we should minister to and interact with people who are non-Christians. Jesus modeled this for us during His time on earth. However, we don't have to put our children in a position to be examples of the gospel. In most cases, they are not ready to handle the pressure of wanting to fit in while holding on to their faith. If we pray and sense a caution about their interactions with a certain person, a show they're watching, or a place they're going, we had better pay attention to it. If something feels off, it probably is. Trust the nudge of the Holy Spirit as it pertains to your child. Remember, the Enemy is crafty. He knows that if he can capture the hearts and minds of our children early, he's in a prime position to continue to influence them. The Bible says it like this: "Be alert and of sober mind. Your enemy the devil prowls around like a roaring lion looking for someone to devour" (1 Peter 5:8).

We would be fooling ourselves to believe that the Enemy wouldn't use anyone or anything to cause our children to stumble. If we truly want to truly model our faith, this may mean some uncomfortable "no" encounters. We will talk about this a bit more later. Nonetheless, we cannot spend our days talking about Jesus only to allow our children to participate in or be around situations that reflect the opposite. This will diminish our ability to witness and will create a sense of confusion within our children. We must never forget that a warrior is willing to do whatever it takes to win the war. In the case of spiritual war against our children, let us be the biggest champions for them, even when others don't understand. We can trust the Holy Spirit to give us complete clarity in who and what will add to their faith and what will cause damage. When all else fails, pray for wisdom—He will certainly answer.

Search Me, Lord

I want to draw you back to Psalm 139:23–24 (NLT): "Search me, O God, and know my heart; test me and know my anxious thoughts. Point out anything in me that offends you, and lead me along the path of everlasting life."

The battle cry of every mother should be, "God, search me!"

The battle cry of every mother should be, "God, search me!" If there is anything in me that must go, remove it. If my actions have caused my child to stumble, show me. Teach me how to think like You, walk in step with Your Spirit, and raise my child in a way that brings You honor." This prayer is a dangerous one, as it reminds us to be accountable. Yet it should bring conviction and not condemnation. We have all fallen short. When it comes to parenting, there is no mother who says all the right things and correctly responds every time. In most cases, it's when we mess up that the Holy Spirit gives us the gentle nudge that we need to do better. Asking God to show us how to be better mothers is not a sign of weakness but a sign of great victory. What great love we are showing when we seek to be better for ourselves and our families. I implore you to pray and ask yourself some real and raw questions today.

1. Am I frustrated all the time?
2. What is the general mood of my home (upbeat, chaotic, overwhelming)?
3. Do I have a habit that might be a stumbling block for my children?
4. How do I respond to disappointment?
5. How have I shared my faith with my children?
6. Do I treat my children like a burden or a blessing?
7. How do I treat people outside my home?
8. Do I gossip? Cheat? Lie?

9. Do I model my faith through studying God's Word and applying it?
10. If my child acted like me, would I want to be around them?
11. Are there influences that I allow that the Lord is causing me to cut off or shift?
12. Does my behavior in public reflect my behavior behind closed doors?

Victorious parenting involves *you* evaluating *you*! Being such an influence in your children's life is a blessing. Make a choice today to exemplify the words Paul spoke to Timothy long ago (1 Timothy 4:12). May your faith be a testimony for your children and your children's children and even their children. A mother who walks out her faith is a powerful force to be reckoned with.

──────────── VICTORY VERSE ────────────

Jesus said, "Let the little children come to me, and do not hinder them, for the kingdom of heaven belongs to such as these." (Matthew 19:14)

──────────── REFLECTIONS ────────────

1. Why do you think it's important to speak and act out the Word to your family?
2. What is something you feel the Holy Spirit is leading you to change today?
3. Read Psalm 37:5. What are some ways you can commit your motherhood journey to the Lord?

──────────── POWER PRAYER ────────────

Lord, I thank You for _____. I praise You for creating them and knowing the intricate details about their lives. Because of this I know I can trust You to lead me completely as a I mother _____. I ask that You give me the words to say and the wisdom to know when to be quiet. Teach me how to model my faith before them. Lord, I repent for the times I have not behaved in a way that reflected You.

Teach me how to treat my children. Show me when I am wrong and need correction. Let my faith be genuine and from the heart and not an act before them. Lord, show me when and how to pray for each child.

Teach me to teach them how to pray. Lord, help me to rightly divide Your word of truth. May the Word come alive in their lives even now. Lead me to Bible stories that remind them of Your goodness and verses that bring life.

Help my relationship with You and knowledge of Your Word be so strong that my faith is immovable. I praise You for the shift in my home. God, if there is anyone or anything that is causing _____ to stumble, reveal it now, Lord. Teach me to be obedient to this, even when it's hard. I pray for wisdom to infiltrate my parenting journey. Help me to walk in discernment and to depend upon You for all things. I surrender my parenting completely to You. In Jesus's name. Amen.

Chapter Ten

TRAIN THEM UP

Experience teaches us that it is much easier to prevent
an enemy from posting themselves than it is to dislodge
them after they have got possession.
GEORGE WASHINGTON

THE MOST QUOTED VERSE ON parenting is nestled in the book of
Proverbs: "Train up a child in the way he should go, even when he
grows older he will not abandon it" (22:6 NASB). I believe parents
hold on to this verse so dearly because of the attached promise that
when their children are old they will "not abandon it [their train-
ing]." There is something about this phrase that brings hope. It's as
if the writer of Proverbs was saying, "Don't worry. It will all work
out in the end. Even if they stray between childhood and old age,
stay hopeful—they will remember what was taught." For many, this
should be a sigh of relief. Yet the beginning of this verse is what
typically causes the tension. How exactly do we "train up" a child?

First we must dive into what it means to train. According to
Strong's Hebrew Lexicon, the phrase "train up" translates to the
word *ḥānak*,[1] which can be defined as the following:

- to help one to understand
- to narrow

- to make one experienced for a task
- to consecrate or make clean

Each of these definitions makes it clear that training is intentional. True training doesn't happen once a month or by happenstance. Instead, when we take on the responsibility to train another person in any skill, it's for a purpose and on purpose.

The Importance of Training

When I think of training, I am reminded of my time working in childcare years ago. For about four years, my role was to lead a classroom with two other teachers and twelve one-year-old children. Although I loved the children, the hardest aspect of handling toddlers was training them to follow directions. The most difficult of these challenges would occur daily around 10:00 a.m. The childcare center was connected to a high-rise building and was massive in size—so much so that the playground wasn't just outside the doors of the classroom. To get to the outdoor facilities, we would have to walk two blocks away from the classroom with all the toddlers in tow. We did so with a long, colorful string of circles called "the rings." The rings were a lifesaver in getting the children to move in one accord. The only thing required to move the group was for each child to hold on to his or her specific circle while walking.

Needless to say, the newly walking children struggled to hold on to the rings without running and to move in the direction of the playground. It would take a month to get a child who never walked with the rings to walk in step with the other children without falling. Even more so, if one little one fell, they all fell like dominoes. Although cute to watch, it certainly was difficult for the teachers and required much patience. A walk that should have taken five minutes could easily take fifteen or twenty. Yet every day was a new opportunity to train the children how to walk while holding on tightly and how to not become so distracted that they went in the wrong direction.

Warrior Mother, this is the perfect example of what God is calling us to do when it comes to training our children. You see, the other teachers and I had to be intentional about how we trained the toddlers to use the rings. We had to set the expectations daily. When one child fell, rather than break his spirit for messing up, we had to scoop him up and give him another opportunity. We also had to be careful to lead them toward the playground and not let them lead us. Occasionally we would have to use a stern voice to catch their attention when they were off course, and our eyes had to stay open to those who were falling behind or those who needed more assistance. For our younger children or those who weren't feeling their best, we even had to be willing to give grace and just hold them until we reached the destination. The rings give us a good picture of the mother's role in training her children. But no matter what, we set the pace and we set the direction. This is what training looks like.

When we think of the verse that admonishes us to train our children, we must know that we are taking on a heavy responsibility. However, our main goal isn't to get our kids to the playground but to lead them closer to the Lord. We must be mindful that we are also training them in everyday matters. From how to manage stress to how to treat others, to how to take care of their own physical health, and more, we teach them how to face the real world with excellence. And finally, we are molding them to be able to stand up against every attack their natural flesh, the world, and the Enemy will throw at them. Our goal is for their whole person—body, soul (mind, will, emotions), and spirit—to be well. Every day may be a different focus. Circumstances, age, and your family dynamics may cause you to home in on one area more than another. No matter what the case may be, you set the pace and the direction.

In other words, in our homes we are called to shepherd. If we're married, we have the privilege of doing this alongside our spouses. In the natural sense, a shepherd takes responsibility for guiding, protecting, and giving care to the sheep in his fold. On their own, sheep cannot find a green pasture or keep themselves safe. They are reliant on the shepherd to guide them to safety and to attend to their needs.

Here's the thing about a shepherd. A shepherd leads. The sheep follow. You will never see it the other way around.

Time and time again, I have seen parents not take this concept to heart. They allow the children to take the lead for what is right and wrong and make major decisions. There is a time and place for this when dealing with older teens. Yet this is certainly not the image of parenting that we see in the Word. Proverbs 22:6 doesn't say, "Just let them figure it out" or "Allow the child to set the pace." Instead, the direction is clear—we are called to take ownership and decide what behaviors are allowed and what goals are essential, and to seek God for a plan in accomplishing His will for our children's lives.

Before we go any further, I want to draw your attention to a few verses that remind us of this truth: Christian parenting is not passive. Let's consider what the Word says about discipline.

> Discipline your children, and they will give you peace; they will bring you the delights you desire. (Proverbs 29:17)

> Children, obey your parents in everything, for this pleases the Lord. (Colossians 3:20)

> Listen, my son, to your father's instruction and do not forsake your mother's teaching. (Proverbs 1:8)

> Love the LORD your God with all your heart and with all your soul and with all your strength. These commandments that I give you today are to be on your hearts. Impress them on your children. Talk about them when you sit at home and when you walk along the road, when you lie down and when you get up. (Deuteronomy 6:5–7)

We are called to see parenting as more than just surviving another day; parenting is a training ground for the battles ahead. Let's be clear, the Enemy has no issue with you not taking parenting seriously. He has no issue with helping your child reach the destination he has in mind—hell! His demons also have no issue planting seeds of doubt, disruption, or confusion in your home. We make his job all too easy when we don't take the job of disciplining our children seriously. Let's not give the Enemy that advantage any longer. Too much is on the line!

God didn't give us children to drop off at the local church and then run, in hopes the pastor could mold them for life. No, much like every soldier must participate in basic training, we must also see our homes as a training ground. Without basic training, the soldiers would have no sense of direction or the standards they are to uphold. Regardless of the military branch, the goal remains the same: to raise up the next group of soldiers who can be ready for the missions to come. This requires that leaders instill a sense of discipline, teaching them to have a sincere love for their new career choice and to have patience and wisdom when falling off track. If we lean into this concept and see our homes as more than just a place to eat, sleep, and hang out together, we can really start to see changes in our homes. Many times we see behavioral issues or an unwillingness to embrace the Christ-centered culture simply because we have not set the structure and pace. We are allowing the children to lead and not the other way around. In the following pages, I want to empower you with practical ways to train up your child in the Lord.

Keys for Discipline

Love is unconditional—approval of poor behavior is not. In fact, the epitome of love is correction. When we care for someone, we desire for them to have the best outcomes. I believe love is the reason so many give unsolicited parenting advice and our own parents and in-laws can't wait to tell us how to raise our children. Love will compel you to speak up and act when another person is in danger physically, spiritually, or emotionally. Proverbs 3:12 (NLT) says it like this: "For the LORD corrects those he loves, just as a father corrects a child in whom he delights."

I would be bold enough to say that the Lord has corrected you here and there. He corrects and even sets a standard of behavior out of His love. Many in the world believe that we serve a controlling God who seeks to rob us of our freedom. They see His commands to live a holy life free from sexual sin, pride, greed, and idolatry as a way to handcuff them. Yet it's quite the opposite. He tells us to stay away from sexual sin, as He knows the pain that comes from giving oneself away without a godly commitment. He tells us to run from pride and greed, as He knows that these two things will lead us to make reckless choices. And He warns us against idolatry as He knows that if we exalt anything before Him, we will always come up empty. The boundaries created by the Lord and the conviction brought when we operate outside of them is the essence of love.

Discipline is not a bad word. Disciplining a child is not something we should run away from but run toward. I can readily admit, however, that this heavy word *discipline* has a bad reputation. Perhaps when you were a child you were spanked harshly for every poor choices. Maybe your home was abusive and you lived in fear of making your parent upset. I don't know your story. Neither am I here to defend what has happened to you in the past. Instead, I want to empower you to understand that discipline may be more practical than you think.

There are a few keys to disciplining that I have seen work when coupled with prayer and the leading of the Holy Spirit.

Key One—Become Aware of Your Parenting Style

Perhaps one the most empowering things you can do is learn your parenting style. The late developmental psychologist Diana Baumrind theorized that each of us fall into one of three major categories: authoritarian, permissive, or authoritative.[2] Theorists E. E. Maccoby and J. A. Martin expanded on Baumrind's theory by including an additional type of parenting style called "uninvolved."[3] Together these four categories of parenting are used as a key way to break down the methods in which one chooses to parent. These styles can be summed up in the following way.

Authoritarian—"Do what I say."
Permissive—"You take the lead; I will follow."
Authoritative—"Do what I say, but I will hear what you have to say."
Uninvolved—"Do as you choose without recourse."

UNINVOLVED
Indifferent
Annoyed
Unresponsive
Disinterested
Too Busy to Parent
Unaware of daily needs
Can become neglectful

PERMISSIVE
Compromising of beliefs
Child empowered to make choices
Attentive
Led by emotion of child
Relationship-driven

AUTHORITATIVE
Balanced between relationship and rules
Assertive
Willing to listen
Led by logic, sometimes leads to compromising
Parent-led choices given

AUTHORITARIAN
Focus on rules
Aggressive approach
Uncompromising
Expects complete compliance
Parent has ultimate say
Can become abusive

The uninvolved parent has no sense of guidance and is indifferent about what happens with the child overall. Prayerfully, you never fall into the category of uninvolved parenting. The uninvolved parent can easily turn into being neglectful. Being too busy to care or failing to pay attention to the daily needs of the child, to be emotionally available, or to set any rules whatsoever can leave you in the uninvolved parenting category. If you found yourself in this category, instead of choosing shame, choose action. I would encourage you to pause and pray for the Lord to show you what may need to be taken off your plate so you can focus on parenting.

The permissive parent allows the child to take the lead on choices in hopes that the child will learn through a series of trial and error. Permissive parenting has benefits in some cases. For instance, this style may be more appropriate for older teens who have shown maturity in their past choices. In these cases, the parent can step back and allow the child to make decisions. Rather than micromanage each choice, the parent can be assured that the child has a good foundation and will most likely have a good outcome. This will set the teenager up to be more successful as he or she leaves home and pursues college. Permissive parenting, on the other hand, can also be negative. This form of parenting also arises when the parents have given up on trying to correct the behavior. The child is allowed to do as he or she chooses due to the parent being intimidated by the child or not wanting to cause more disruption within the home. This is a risky position as a parent, as you give up the right to discipline the child when you allow them to be the ultimate authority. A child should never be the shepherd of your home.

In general, authoritative parenting has been considered the most effective style of parenting. The authoritative parent takes the balanced approach to set the rules but is willing to hear input and make changes with time. This form of parenting has a clear set of rules, but the parents are open to change as well. According to the Michigan State University Extension program, homes that demonstrate authoritative parenting tend to have children who are "responsible, able to manage their aggression, have high self-esteem and are very self-confident."[4] The reason authoritative parenting is seen as the best balance is that it still allows the parent to lead while valuing the worth of the child. You can see this form of leading others in the way Jesus responded to His disciples. Yes, He spoke truth and great wisdom to them. However, He also asked His disciples questions to learn more about what they were feeling about situations. In doing so, He gained their respect and their trust.

Authoritative parents will often present children with specific choices and allow them to make the best decision. In this way, children are empowered to make choices that fall in line with the rules of the home and are based on what is morally right. In doing so, they develop a sense of independence and trust that their parents have their best interests at heart. This parenting style balances setting firm rules and having an active relationship with the child.

Authoritarian, the final parenting style, is one that is focused on rules and behavior management. Those with the authoritarian style tend to create a home that has a heavy focus on rules. Following the rules is first and foremost. Having a relationship with the child is an added benefit, if it occurs. Few choices are given in an authoritarian home. What the parents say goes—there is no option or debate, only complete compliance. Parents are often willing to do whatever is deemed necessary to see their children behave appropriately. We often see this form of parenting with parents of young children or with children who have behaved poorly in the past. This parent is effective in quickly changing disruptive and challenging behavior. The authoritarian parent takes the role as the drill sergeant seeking to get the troops in line. Perfection is required and expected. Unfortunately, this form of parenting can also create a tense environment, where yelling and spankings become daily occurrences.

Authoritarian parents inadvertently use fear to get the children in line. Sadly, this creates a sense of panic and anxiety within children when they mess up. Before long a home can go from being a loving environment to one where children are "walking on eggshells" to keep the parent happy. Children in these homes tend to be timid and nervous about making choices for fear of what may happen to them. In some cases, they may even become rebellious from the frustration of the rigidness of the home. If your parenting style is authoritarian, you must be careful to ensure that your desire for rules isn't over-riding the beauty of forming relationships with your children. If such parents aren't careful, authoritarian homes can be just as detrimental to the child's development as uninvolved parenting.

Parents tend to fall on the spectrum of one of these parenting styles. At any given time, or even based on the age of the child, we may swing in and out of these styles. Learning your parenting style empowers you to know the tone that is set in your home. If you have multiple children, it can also highlight where you may be showing favoritism. For instance, if you tend to be permissive with one child but authoritarian with another, children will definitely notice. I have found that before we can tackle discipline in the home, we must first take an inventory of how we parent overall.

The parenting style will set the atmosphere of the home. Consider your parenting style as your home's thermostat. The uninvolved parent's home will likely be cold and/or neglectful (leading to unruliness), and the authoritarian parent's home will likley be run with fiery passion and intensity (leading to much tension). Let us be mindful of the temperature of our homes and quickly correct moments that feel out of control. If you find that your parenting has turned cold, take a moment and pray about how you can add more intention and care. In the same way, if your home has become intense like a mini boot camp, take time to calm down and see how you can soften your approach. The Lord can give wisdom on how to find balance in this area if we are willing to seek Him.

Key Two—Establish a Clear Set of Rules

What are the rules of your home? Do you have a set bedtime? Does each child have specific chores? Is running indoors allowed? How long are electronics allowed each day? What kind of relationships are allowed with the opposite sex? When must homework be completed? The answers to such questions should be known by everyone in the home. There should be no confusion over the expectation. If you can't define the expectations of your home clearly, neither can your child.

Simply put, you cannot expect children to follow rules that you have not set. Many times children misbehave because you haven't set the standard. One week they may be allowed to skip chores entirely, and the next week they may get in trouble for not completing them. One day they may be allowed to use electronics all day, and the next they may only get to play with them in the morning. As a mother of seven, I have struggled in this area. Yet it's important that the rules be clear, concise, and easy to understand. When they are constantly changing, we cannot hold children accountable for them. Some parents establish these rules by having a rule chart within the home. Others make a habit of having a family meeting to remind the children of what is expected. Whatever you decide to do, be sure there is no confusion.

When it comes to parenting, write the vision and make it plain. If you have failed to communicate the vision and expectations of the home, use the moments when things go wrong to set the expectation rather than punish. You shouldn't punish a child for what you failed to explain. Simply put, we cannot expect children to just know better. If we've never told them *not to do it*, we can expect *they will do it* when the opportunity arises. The more we give them the knowledge of what is morally right and acceptable in our homes, the more they can work to improve their behavior. Remember, we are called to instruct them. Sharing the expectation is the easiest but most important aspect of discipline.

Key Three—Teach the Importance of Choices

Our choices matter. From an early age, children should be taught that every choice will elicit a positive or negative response. When we teach children this concept, we ingrain in them that they have the power to make choices and get results. They can either earn what they desire or receive an unwanted response. In most cases, the choice is theirs concerning what will happen next for them. One way to teach this quickly is by introducing choices often. For example, suppose you're taking a five-year-old prone to tantrums into the grocery store. Your instructions to your child could sound a little like this:

> "Liam, we are about to go into the grocery store. I know this is not always your favorite place. When we go into the store, you need to make good choices. I expect you to sit in the cart and use your inside voice. This is the right choice to make. If you choose not to do this, when we get home, you will not get a treat. You will go straight to naptime. The choice is completely yours to behave in the store or to miss out on a treat and take a nap. Do you understand?"

After this choice-led conversation, having the child repeat the two choices alerts you that he or she is completely aware of the consequences attached to his or her future choices. From here, you can go into the store knowing that your child understands the expectations and will be able to see in real time the power of choice. Thus, the child holds the responsibility of making the right choice. In this scenario, if Liam chooses to have a tantrum, the mom can easily remind him that it was his choice to misbehave. Losing the treat when he returns home and having to take a nap were a result of his actions and not his mom's. This teaches the child responsibility. I have seen this work with a child as young as three all the way to an older teen. The pattern of clear choices and immediate responses empowers you and the child and reminds him or her that every action will cause a positive or negative consequence. Just as the Bible says, "'I have the right to do anything,' you say—but not everything is beneficial. 'I have the right to do anything'—but not everything is constructive" (1 Corinthians 10:23). Life will be a series of choices for our children, from how they behave in school to whom they will date, to accepting Jesus as the Lord of their lives! Let's teach our children early that some choices will reap amazing rewards and others will lead to great harm. Learning the value of making good choices is a vital part of discipline and will certainly help them as the Enemy tempts them later in life.

Key Four—Have a Clear Response to Choices

Concerning behavior modification, consider the principle I call "like it or loathe it." Every response you have toward your children's behavior needs to fall within the paradigm of this phrase. Let me explain.

To decrease a behavior, you have two choices:

- take away what they like or
- add what they loathe.

To increase a behavior, you have two choices,

- add what they like or
- take away what they loathe.

Any behavior will elicit a response that is appropriate for the specific child and scenario. The more we pay attention to our children and their likes and dislikes, we can easily pick up what will work for them.

1. Decreasing Unwanted Behavior

    Unwanted behaviors are a symptom of a lack of understanding or care for the consequences. Discipline is our way of helping children to care about their choices and to understand that every action counts. To decrease a behavior, we must home in on the concept of negative consequences. Using the like concept of like it or loathe it, you must first take an inventory of things they like to do or participate in. Does your four-year-old love getting stickers when she does a good job? Does your preteen enjoy hanging out with friends after school? Removing either of these desires would be considered taking away what they like. When using this form of punishment, let's not take away things that are long-lasting and positive for their spiritual growth or that can never be replaced. For instance, unless the situation was extreme, you would likely not ban your child from youth group or attending his or her prom. Punishments like these break a child's spirit, which is not the goal.

Another option is adding what they loathe. Having the child do something he or she dislikes will bring swift correction. If you have a teenage son who despises doing dishes, an adequate punishment for not cleaning his room could be having to do the dishes more days than normal. For the younger child who doesn't like isolation, having him sit in a reflection chair to think about his choice or lie in bed for a few moments while calming down will likely elicit a response. Their disdain of the punishment should discourage him or her from the unwanted behavior. Eventually you will reach the point that just mentioning the loathed action will lead the child to correct his or her actions. Again, the goal is not to break the child with harsh labor or things that will crush his or her spirit. I am a firm believer that a few tears shed are okay. Abuse, neglect, and causing intentional harm are not.

Discipline is simply to set off an alarm that what's being done is not allowed in your home. Even more so, when we set the tone for following rules and honor in our home, children will be more likely to do the same in the outside world. Sadly, not following rules in the real world will come with major consequences, from school suspension to jail to even death.

Again, correction is an act of love and a source of protection. We do our children a great disservice when we don't create boundaries of what it means to follow rules.

2. Celebrating Good Behavior

It is extremely important that we not only punish the bad

but celebrate the good. Your child should become accustomed to hearing praises for a job well done. Just as much as punishments decrease unwanted behaviors, so do rewards! The like it or loathe it works well when celebrating good behavior. When a child does well, we can give him what he loves. This doesn't have to be a tangible object. It can be a compliment or even a hug. It can also be an earned reward, like a trip to the dollar store for young children or a night out with friends for teenagers.

Whatever the case may be, we should rejoice when our children are doing well. We can also take away something they loathe. For instance, suppose the same child from my earlier example who hates doing dishes gets straight As. Maybe that would warrant a week without dishes. In this way, we say, "I see you trying and I'm proud of you." We must realize that children naturally desire to please their parents. When they put forth their greatest effort only for it to be ignored, we can expect they will become indifferent about their good behavior. Although doing the right thing should be an expectation, we should make a habit of praising our children. Make a habit of catching your child being good!

3. Mixing Up Your Responses

Children are resilient. In most cases, this is a remarkable thing. Yet when it comes to changing behavior, this attribute can make discipline tough. A time will come when they become accustomed to the negative consequences of their actions. For instance, suppose your go-to punishment for your teenager is taking away video game time. If this becomes a daily punishment, eventually your teenager will no longer be affected. In fact, he will think, *She's going to take away my video games. No big deal.* And the poor choice will not be taken seriously. If not cleaning his room, not being kind to a sibling, or not getting good grades *only* takes away his favorite video game, this is a risk he is willing to take. Whenever your child reaches the point of thinking, *What's the worst that can happen?*, you know it's time to switch things up. We should be consistent with enforcing the rules and disciplining poor behavior. However, we need to be flexible and creative in the methods we choose.

4. Disciplining with Care

When it comes to discipline, we should never correct our children in anger or retaliation, or in a way that would be deemed abusive. Unfortunately, the Bible doesn't give specific instructions on how to discipline. Even the commonly used verse of Proverbs 13:24, "Whoever spares the rod hates their children" (often misquoted as "Spare the rod and spoil the child"), is one that reminds us of the rod used by a shepherd. A shepherd's rod was a tool used to bring correction, not to issue pain. In his article "Is Spanking Biblical?," Dr. Daniel Huerta, vice president of parenting and youth for Focus on the Family, breaks down the above verse in the following way: "Rarely, a shepherd needs to use his rod to correct or protect his sheep. It's not punishment out of anger, but rather a protective mechanism to keep the sheep from danger. It's correction out of concern and love."[5]

Whether through time-outs, taking things away, or even a smack on the hand for a child who may be putting himself in danger, how you discipline is an individual decision for your home. Whatever you choose, it's important that you as a parent are mature enough to handle your anger and have self-control. Even with the controversial topic of spanking, there are certainly more studies that argue against spanking than for it. If we aren't careful, spanking can increase aggression, break the child's spirit, or lead him or her to being afraid of a parent. We should desire our children to respect us, not to walk in terror—there is a difference. Again, our goal should never be to inflict severe pain or cause injury. If you feel like you've lost control, chances are you have. If you feel like you will lose control, chances are you will. Remember, discipline is an opportunity for redirection, not an excuse to cause pain. You can easily implement course correction without ever needing to hit, raise your voice, or ruin your child's self-esteem. Instead, practice prayer, strategy, and consistency. It's challenging but possible.

Key Five—Practice Patience

Patience is a quintessential aspect of discipline. When we deal with children, we must remember that they will not always be perfect. They will miss the mark and make mistakes in areas that they once mastered. If we're honest, we mothers mess up and fall short daily. I often imagine the Father in heaven shaking His head at me and thinking, *I thought I already handled this situation with her!* Whether you struggle with pride, idolatry, pornography, anger, or jealousy, I can assure you that you are in daily need of a Savior. So although we may desire to have perfectly behaved children, let us never become too far removed from realizing we are in daily need of grace ourselves. We can choose to be kind when we want to be furious and speak gently when we want to yell. Just as we want our children to have self-control, a vital aspect of being a godly disciplinarian is to know when to respond with punishment and when to respond with grace.

> **Just as we want our children to have self-control, a vital aspect of being a godly disciplinarian is to know when to respond with punishment and when to respond with grace.**

Let us remember that when we bring correction, it is out of our love for our children. I end this chapter with reminding you of what true love is. Our ultimate desire is that our children would come to know the Lord. May the way we discipline reflect the love of our Father in heaven and not become a tool for the Enemy to sow discord in our homes. Godly discipline should reflect His love. "Love is patient, love is kind. It does not envy, it does not boast, it is not proud. It does not dishonor others, it is not self-seeking, it is not easily angered, it keeps no record of wrongs. Love does not delight in evil but rejoices with the truth. It always protects, always trusts, always hopes, always perseveres" (1 Corinthians 13:4–7).

Train them in love.

Be consistent.

Be patient.

Trust God for every step in between.

─────────────── VICTORY VERSE ───────────────

Start children off on the way they should go, and even when they are old they will not turn from it. (Proverbs 22:6)

─────────────── REFLECTIONS ───────────────

1. How does the Lord's correction prove His love for you?
2. Which parenting style describes you the most? How has this been reflected in your parenting?
3. What are the most important rules of your home? What have you done to increase or decrease the chances of these rules being followed?

─────────────── POWER PRAYER ───────────────

Lord, I thank You for blessing me to be the mother of _____. I recognize that I must take ownership of this important mission. I ask for help in raising them in a way that honors You, Lord. Father, teach me how to train them up. I stand on the promise that they shall not depart from Your Word. I believe for their salvation even now. Lord, I pray that You teach me the way You would like me to discipline _____. Show me creative ways to bring forth change that won't break their spirits. If I've been harsh in the past or my discipline has not reflected Your love, I ask that You forgive me. I recognize that just as I am training them to face the battles ahead, You are also training me. Help me to receive Your correction. God, I thank You that You are so patient with me. Show me when I'm being impatient with _____. I ask that You be the foundation of my home. May I parent in peace and not out of my own frustration or fear. Lord, help me to be levelheaded as I deal with my children and not be led by emotion or retaliation. I pray against strife and tension in my home as we institute these new principles. Show me how to love my children well and choose grace over retribution. Lord, I love You and praise You for being with me every step of the way. I trust You for full wisdom when it comes to discipline. In Jesus's name. Amen.

Chapter Eleven

MORALE MATTERS

An army's effectiveness depends on its size, training,
experience, and morale, and morale is worth more than
any of the other factors combined.

NAPOLEON BONAPARTE

I WILL NEVER FORGET THAT call: "We're being stationed in Mobile,
Alabama." After waiting weeks to hear my husband's voice while he
was at boot camp, this call was beyond exciting. My mind started to
wonder how important his role would be in the US military. Would
he be saving lives, making important choices, protecting the borders?
I couldn't wait to hear about what my guy would be doing to serve
his country. After his first day on the job, he arrived home to tell me
about the duty station and his responsibilities. That I wasn't expecting what he had to say would be an understatement. Out of all the
possible jobs, his role was to work in the MWR (Morale Welfare
Recreation) shop as a cashier. His entire day would be spent helping
people rent tools and sports equipment. When asked what this could
possibly have to do with the mission of the Coast Guard, he replied in
a rather blunt tone, "The military guys need things to do so they can
have fun, or they'll lose their minds, maybe even hurt themselves."

Over time I saw more and more how the MWR shop was a valuable resource. Although it felt insignificant compared to rescuing
people in peril or keeping the coast safe, I realized how protecting

the mental state of the military members was a crucial mission. Providing opportunities for the men and women in uniform to have fun and community was indeed an essential job that someone needed to step up and do. Quite frankly, it doesn't matter how well trained a person is for a battle—if her spirit is broken, she will always struggle when it's time to fight.

As moms, we must recognize that this concept is the same for the troops within our homes. We can teach them the Word. We can carry them to church. We can even help them memorize Scripture to stand up to the devil. However, if we never consider the overall culture of our homes and the atmosphere being cultivated, we can expect that our efforts will not go far. Many times our parenting focuses on behavior modification. The goal becomes raising upstanding citizens; a bonus is if they love the Lord. But I want to submit to you that caring for the hearts of our children is just as important, perhaps more important.

Warrior Mothers Lead Their Tribe into Victory

Consider this: soldiers who are wounded emotionally will always struggle to keep up mentally and physically. No matter how much they've been trained for battle, they will always come up short. Perhaps the daunting idea that they don't measure up to the other soldiers will cause them to overcompensate in battle and take unnecessary risks. Maybe the pressure of needing to move up in rank to impress their superiors causes them to go into deep depression or even to take their own lives. Their inability to carry the emotional weight of their lives will make them liabilities rather than assets when struggles come. And although their military chain of command may teach them how to operate well during a physical battle, their everyday lives may be one of great defeat.

In the same way, if you haven't been intentional about attending to the emotional well-being of your children, they, too, may be silently hurting. Depending on the age of the child, it may not always be easy to recognize when he or she needs extra love and care. However, if we pay close attention, we can discern times when he or she needs us more than ever. Here's what I've learned in life. There is a difference between not *knowing* and not *noticing*. Although we may not always know what's going on, God can give us insight and wisdom to know when something isn't quite right, so notice the need and act. Here are a few telltale signs that our children aren't just in need of extra prayer but of intentional moments of love and care as well.

- Withdrawal from peers
- Sudden disinterest in activities once loved
- Sudden resistance to wanting to be hugged
- Speaking poorly about themselves
- Overall depressive state
- Anxiousness, overwhelming fear, night terrors
- Outbursts of tears or more sensitive than normal
- Refusing to speak or share what's wrong
- Uncontrolled anger
- Pushing of previously established boundaries
- Acting out in public and/or in school
- Disrespectfulness
- Bullying of others
- Feeling like they are to blame
- Inability to control emotions and calm down
- Violence
- Always speaking with their head down or with a sense of guilt

Any combination of these signs should set off an alarm. When I notice any of these in my home, I immediately think of a phrase popularized by law enforcement: "Man down! Man down!" This short statement is an alert to everyone that someone is hurt and needs help immediately. Take note that the behaviors above act as a siren to notify us that something is wrong. We can either actively respond to these warnings or passively allow days to go by with the hurt piling up. In some cases, we attribute the change of behavior to personality or puberty. In most cases, however, this is not the truth. The reality is this: the Enemy and his demonic forces are good at their job. The Bible says it like this: "Stay alert! Watch out for your great enemy, the devil. He prowls around like a roaring lion, looking for someone to devour" (1 Peter 5:8 NLT).

The Enemy knows that if he can break your child's spirit, he can disrupt the entire home. Before long, your child will interpret every scenario as being unloved, and you will be left feeling like an inadequate parent. This cycle will continue until you battle in prayer (and action), give up, or the child outright rebels. When we recognize low morale early, we can seek the Lord for how to fix it. Note that children experience stress just like adults do. I've heard parents say (and have been guilty of saying) words like, "What do you have to be stressed about?" and "You have everything—why would you be complaining?" But little do we know that the school bully might have said something that haunts them daily. Or they might still be hurting from the loss of a grandparent years prior. Or they might feel overwhelmed by schools and chores. If they have siblings, they may yearn for more attention, for which the lack has left them feeling insignificant.

The difference between childhood stress and adult stress is that children are not always able to express their emotions or fix their circumstances. If finances are low in the home, they can't search for a new job. If the school bully won't leave them alone, they can't un-enroll themselves from school and sign up to be homeschooled. If their parents are constantly arguing, they can't jump in to provide counseling. What is an average amount of stress for adults may be magnified for some children. Our job isn't to belittle their experience but to bear witness to the times they need more support.

Truthfully, when your children are hurting emotionally, it may take weeks or even months to see them overcome the pain of it all. In some cases, the trauma of abuse, the death of a loved one, or the divorce of a parent may require a counselor to see them find peace again. However, my heart for you is that you can be proactive in your motherhood journey rather than succumbing to reactive responses. If we are intentional about the morale of our homes, we can help facilitate the healing process and be a source of hope for our children.

Ultimately, our source and our children's primary source for faith and hope is the Lord. Yet we are called to be a resource to help them experience the love of God right here on earth. God is the perfect example of how we can be intentional and notice the silent cries for emotional help.

"The LORD is close to the brokenhearted and saves those who are crushed in spirit" (Psalm 34:18). And we also know that God uses the way we've been comforted to comfort others. Second Corinthians 1:3–4 tells us, "Praise be to the God and Father of our Lord Jesus Christ, the Father of compassion and the God of all comfort, who comforts us in all our troubles, so that we can comfort those in any trouble with the comfort we ourselves receive from God."

God's love notices us even in our weakest moments. God's love draws us to Him. God's love is our resting place when we are burdened. I am convinced that the way we comfort and create a loving atmosphere will be one of our greatest victories in motherhood. There are several key aspects we should consider when caring for the morale of our children: giving encouragement, the power of our words, nurturing their gifting, being available, and providing opportunities for genuine fun. Let's take a moment to explore what these can look like in your home.

Giving Encouragement

We should be our children's biggest encouragers. From encouraging them on the field during a sports game to being kind when they experience a disappointment or struggle with grades, your role is to show up and let them know you are their biggest fan. I once heard it like this: "At any given moment you are your child's greatest cheerleader or coach." For younger children, your role is coach. You call the plays, you help direct the path, you give the instruction, you correct when things don't go right, and you reward the big wins. For the older children and young adults, you are the cheerleader. Though you cannot dictate the moves, you can show up, you can motivate, you can announce their wins, and you can be a comfort when things go wrong. As a mother of children in sports, I want to tell you that both coaching and cheerleading are important and a privilege. Notice, we are not called to be a drill instructor barking orders, but one who meets our children with instructions and comfort.

In modern society, there are enough people speaking negative words over our children. Even if it's not said directly, they can easily look at social media and any comment section to learn exactly what people may perceive about their race, gender, religion, or political beliefs. Our job is to counteract the constant noise of the world around them with the truth about who our children are. We can use our words and actions to break the cycle of negativity and remind them daily that they are loved. When we show up daily with love, we can expect that when things get tough, Mom will be the first person they run to. Your child should know that if no one else supports them, you do!

If no one else believes in them, you will!

If no one else will pray for them, you will!

If no one else has a positive word on a tough day, you do!

If no one else can forgive, you can!

If no one else will pray for them, you're ready!

If no one else will challenge them in love, you will!

Proverbs 31:26 (NASB) says, "She opens her mouth with wisdom, and the teaching of kindness is on her tongue." In other words, wisdom and kindness are what we should be known for. We won't always approve of the behavior and the choices our children make. They will certainly cause frustration, and we may have to dig deep to find words of encouragement on difficult days. Yet despite all else, we are called to be walking, talking, living, breathing examples of God's love toward our children. God's love is unconditional. His love is kind. His love is patient. His loves sees the best in us. The Lord is calling us to establish a culture where His love leads our every interaction and word that we use toward and about our children.

The Power of Words

According to John 6:63, God's words are spirit and life. I want to draw your attention to the original translation of the words *spirit* and *life*. The word *spirit* is derived from the Greek word *pneûma*, meaning "breath" or "from the nostril." In other words, God's words represent His very breath. The same breath that gave life to Adam and Eve is what empowers His Word. His words don't lead to death but to life. Interestingly, the word "life" in John 6:63 is translated from the word *zōē*, which means "to be active, vibrant, and alive." John 6:63 also reminds us that Scripture is God-breathed, bringing active vibrant life to the hearer! This is powerful and provides a road map for mothers to imitate. Before we utter another phrase toward our children, let us say this in our hearts: *May my words reflect God's Spirit and give life.*

Out of a mother's mouth can flow a sea of encouragement or a well of discouragement. We get to choose. More than anyone else's voice on earth, it's the words of the mother that will reverberate in the heart. The sound and influence of the mother's voice is so powerful that several fire-alarm companies have added a setting that allows a mother's voice to function as an alert in an emergency. In a study at Nationwide Children's Hospital of Columbus, it was found that "kids who heard their mother's voice in an alarm woke up in around two seconds. It took them only about 20 seconds more to take a pre-arranged escape route. Those who heard the standard smoke alarm often took over two minutes to rouse and nearly five minutes to escape. In a real fire, that extra time could spell the difference between life and death, the researchers say."[1]

As I came across this study, I couldn't help but be reminded of how much power our voices have. Our voices can speak life or death. They can settle our children's spirits or cause them to feel insecure. Take a moment of self-reflection and ask yourself a few challenging questions using the following chart. Place a check mark on the side of the word that resembles how you typically interact with those in your home. If needed, create a separate one for each child, as your interactions may be different based on age and your relationship with each child's temperament.

	Encouraging vs. Discouraging	
	Gentle vs. Yelling	
	Uplifting vs. Demeaning	
	Caring vs. Nonchalant	
	Attentive vs. Annoyed	
	Compassionate vs. Callous	
	Considerate vs. Selfish	
	Honoring vs. Dishonoring	
	Praising vs. Humiliating	
	Humble vs. Prideful	
	Forgiving vs. Bitter	

He gives us each day as an opportunity to start over and try again.

My prayer is that the Lord will illuminate areas where you are using His words to show love. If you find that you have more checks on the right side, I want to encourage you. The Lord is gracious. He is well aware of the temperament of your child, your personal life experience, and the situations that may make loving through your language difficult. However, He gives us each day as an opportunity to start over and try again. In some cases God also gives us the wisdom to know when we should choose silence over speaking altogether. Every situation will require a different response. I love what Jesus says about how He should speak and operate: "For I did not speak on my own, but the Father who sent me commanded me to say all that I have spoken" (John 12:49).

Warrior Mother, we must remember that God is our ultimate authority. Our lives and our tongues must be in such alignment with Him that we say only what the Lord says and how He tells us to say it. This can be hard because we are deeply connected to our children emotionally. Deep down we may *feel* like we have all the answers and solutions. We may even feel that we have earned the right to say what we choose to our children. This couldn't be further from the truth. Remember, these are not our children but the Lord's. Rather than fall into this trap of the Enemy to use our tongues without recourse, we should pause frequently and speak when necessary. Often I ask myself, Is there a better way to share what I'm about to say? Time and time again, I've heard the Holy Spirit nudge me and encourage me to say something completely different or nothing at all. There is true victory in slowing down and asking the Lord how to respond and when.

I've even found that for some situations words may not be necessary, only prayer. It would be better to be silent than to use your words to inflict pain. Although a popular phrase says, "Silence is violence," just the opposite is typically true. Silence is often not violence but wisdom. In most cases, we yell and say things we regret because we open our mouths too fast. Remember, we are to be our children's greatest encouragers. We cannot be so when we allow anger, pride, or our own insecurity to guide our tongues. May our words reflect the Spirit of the Lord only. This is how we create atmospheres where we are a safe place for our children. Being a champion for your child means guarding your mouth from saying words that leave him or her crushed. "With the tongue we praise our Lord and Father, and with it we curse human beings, who have been made in God's likeness. Out of the same mouth come praise and cursing. My brothers and sisters, this should not be" (James 3:9–10).

Nurturing Their Gifting

Another way to increase the morale of the those in your home is to nurture your children's giftings. Years ago I worked with a Chinese American woman who shared with me a custom from her upbringing called *Zhuazhou*. In this ancient custom, during the child's first birthday party he or she would be placed in a room with various objects representing a career path, ranging from a stethoscope, to money, to a pen. For instance, an apple could represent a future in agriculture. With little input from the parents, the child would be placed in the middle of the objects and given free will to choose one. In this tradition, it was believed that this choice at an early age was a sign of the child's natural inclination toward a certain profession.

Although most Christians don't institute traditions like these, we have all observed how children's interests tend to be piqued in certain areas at an early age. My oldest would sing all day and even through the night at age one. She now records music. My middle child, by age two, would build large structures using blocks, boxes, and whatever he could put his hands on. Years later he still wants to be a builder. My fifth child took a liking to music and at a very early age would cry when he couldn't touch the church piano or drums. At the age of six, when asked, he will proudly say, "When I grow up, I'm gonna be a Jesus singer." Things could change over time, but it's apparent that if we nurture and provide opportunities for our children, they will continue to grow in their natural giftings.

A part of creating a loving culture is to have the eyes to see who God has called your children to be. In fact, it would be the opposite of love to try to force a certain sport, instrument, and career path on them that they despise. This is what leaves children feeling like they can never be good enough for their parent. If we aren't careful, we can fall into the trap of training our children based on what we wished for own lives. This is a selfish way of thinking and will cause them to be broken in spirit.

I witnessed this with my own child years ago. As a person who is musical, I've always wanted my children to love to play instruments, even though I could not. When the local military base gave the opportunity for a parent-child guitar class, I was the first to sign up.

Needless to say, my twelve-year-old daughter was not pleased, as she had frequently expressed her disdain for playing instruments. She hated every aspect of the class with a passion. Yet every week I insisted that if she kept trying, she would eventually love it. Before long, the commute to the class that I hoped would ignite her desire for instruments turned into a tear-filled ride every week. Not only did this class show her how much she hated playing an instrument, but it also sowed a seed of distrust from her to me. In forcing my will onto her, I showed her that my feelings were more important than her own. Midway through the guitar classes, the Lord convicted me of my behavior and led me to cancel the remaining courses.

Here's what I've learned—if we don't provide opportunities for our children, the Enemy will. Our job is to seek the Lord to learn what they may be yearning to do and find realistic ways to make it happen. Is there a way for your child who loves to dance to take a ballet class? Could your child who enjoys sports participate in a sports summer camp? Motherhood is not about exhausting our bank accounts or every ounce of energy to take our children from activity to activity. Just by seeing the desire and encouraging them to talk about and dream about their dreams can be more than enough to see God move.

Children want to know that their parents believe in them, even when no one else does. In my own home, it's not always practical to have children enrolled in their every desire. The question is, what can I do right now to see them reach their highest potential? Perhaps for the child who likes to bake, you can buy a few cookbooks and supplies and task him with cooking a dish once a week. For the child who loves sports, you could have a weekly playdate with other students who love the same game. For the youth who loves music, you can save money for music software or encourage her to try out for the church worship band. I can assure you that for anything they are interested in, you can find a YouTube video or book that can aid them in learning the craft. It's not about the amount of money you spend but the intention. A child who's focused on his or her passion will have far less time to get into trouble, will be more likely to feel a sense of worth, and will be excited about life. This is how you build children's morale and remind them they are loved.

Being Available

Children need parents who are emotionally available. When I grew up, this was not a common concept. Children were to be seen and not heard. A child's opinion was often downplayed or seen as an excuse to get out of a chore. I implore you not to let this be the tone of your home. For those with teens especially, we must make a choice to listen and respond. There will be times when we don't like or agree with their stances, but we cannot allow pride to convince us that we are always right. Just as our Father in heaven allows for us to share our hearts, we shouldn't be quick to dismiss our children as they share their emotions. I want to caveat this with the recognition that there will be some topics that are not open for discussion—let your no be no in these moments. Similarly, allowing them to share their hearts is never an excuse for them to raise their voices or show disrespect. It's up to you to set the boundary for what this looks like in your home.

Nonetheless, our job is to make space for our children to share how they feel. Oftentimes we learn how our children feel when they are extraordinarily angry. This is because we have never opened the floor for them to share previously. So when they reach their boiling point, they simply explode. My heart is that you would get into a habit of doing an emotional welfare check. I often pull my children aside and ask them simple questions like, "Is there anything bothering you lately?" or "How can I help you in this area?" I have to be honest; I don't always agree with their responses. Yet I am teaching them that I am a safe place for everyday scenarios so that when tough battles come, they can trust me. We cannot afford to ignore the value of being a place of comfort and a listening ear. This gives our children the opportunity to share their emotional struggles and us a chance to explain our reasoning or even to apologize. Here a few phrases that can help to empower you in these moments of vulnerability.

- "Thank you for sharing that."
- "I'm sorry you feel this way."
- "That does sound overwhelming."
- "Is there anything I can do to help you?"
- "I remember when I felt this way too."
- "What you're expressing is common for many children your age."
- "How can I pray for you about this?"

All of these phrases are a reminder to your children that you are walking with them. They also remind you to pause and empathize with them instead of simply giving them solutions or getting angry. Let us be slow to speak, quick to listen, and slow to get angry in these moments. These are the times that can make or break your relationship with your child. Remember, if you aren't creating a healthy relationship with your children, the Enemy will certainly send someone else along who does not have their best interests in mind. Embrace the tough conversations, and know they are a step toward seeing your children grow to their greatest potentials.

Intentional Fun

Time with family should be fun. Unfortunately, the busyness of life can lead us away from simply enjoying togetherness. This is another tactic of the Enemy. Before long we can become so busy trying to make money or to simply survive among the pressures of life that we miss our children's entire childhood. A valuable aspect of morale is being available to spend time together. Quality time goes beyond being in the same room. It is the choice to say I want to put away all other distractions to enjoy your company.

It is never too late to institute a culture of togetherness. Depending on the age of your child and dynamics of your work and family, this may look different from day to day and year to year. It can also vary from child to child. Again, much like nurturing you child's gift, it's not about how much you spend but about the intention behind it. Intentional fun for a five-year-old can look like taking her to the grocery store to choose her favorite cereal or dinner food. (I have learned that younger children require little to be happy. They are just as happy at the local arcade as they are at Disney World.) Being intentional for a ten-year-old may consist of a family game night. And for a teen, fun may be a one-on-one dinner. A walk on a nature trail, a movie night, going to see a sports game, or going out for ice cream are just a few practical ways to tell your child "I love you." In a world that is so busy, let us be willing to slow down for the laughter and joy that come with being intentional about your family. This will be good for their souls and yours!

Facing Your Childhood

Your own childhood will set the tone for how you interact with your children. Growing up in an environment that was unloving, critical, or dismissive may make it difficult for you to relate to the ideas discussed in this chapter. Maybe you were raised in a home where children were to be seen and not heard. Perhaps your home had a parent who was abusive or didn't see the best in you. Maybe getting a hug or encouraging word from your family was rare. Your home may have felt more like a prison with two supervising guards rather than a place of nurturing. The truth is, we all enter parenting with our own "stuff." And although you deeply love your child, your natural inclination may not be to be soft or warm. I've even talked to mothers who shared that it feels uncomfortable to give a gentle embrace to their children. Without experiencing this intentional love, it can take years to learn how to do so from an authentic place. If we aren't careful, our parenting will become a reflection of our own inner pain.

I want to implore you to be the change. In chapter 8 we talked about the power of generational influence. Many elements of your upbringing (good and bad) likely impact you now. Making the change to no longer be controlled by the dysfunctional patterns of your own parents may not come easy. But you can choose to be different. You can choose to let the way you parent be an example of God's love. You may need a daily dose of humility to recognize that you may not always have all the answers. Chances are that you might not always recognize the pain your children may be experiencing. You may not know how to see them live out God's plan for their lives. On your own, you may struggle to figure out how to uplift their spirits when times get tough. There are a lot of unknowns when it comes to raising emotionally healthy children.

Here's the thing—we can get frustrated by the uncertainty or praise God for what we know to be true. We know that we have a God who still speaks to mothers. Again, we know that if we ask for wisdom, God will not rebuke us (James 1:5). We have a God who cares about the well-being of His children. We have a God who is there for us mothers and for our children, to bring comfort in times of frustration. As long as we are surrendered to God, we can have nurturing homes where God's love is tangible. Every step, action, word, and choice must be surrendered. Completely, utterly, unapologetically surrendered to the Lord. And the great news is this—you don't need a psychology degree to foster an emotionally healthy child who can stand strong against the weight of the world. All you need is the Lord's voice and your willingness to show up with love and intention. This is how we can help our children show up to every battle with steady minds and hearts that aren't broken. This is how we can see lives change and how we can see the stifling of the Enemy's plans against our children. Some battles are won with strategy and others by simply winning over the heart.

Notice the needs of your children.

Encourage them like you're the world's greatest cheerleader.

Nurture their giftings.

Have the tough conversations.

Make your family a priority by having fun.

Pray for wisdom on how to do all the above like their lives depends on it.

──────────── VICTORY VERSE ────────────

If you need wisdom, ask our generous God, and he will give it to you. He will not rebuke you for asking. (James 1:5 NLT)

──────────── REFLECTIONS ────────────

1. Have you noticed any of the warning signs that your children may be having a tough time emotionally? Have you responded to this is a way that is reflective of God's heart toward them?
2. Which area do you feel you can improve upon? Encouragement, nurturing their gifts, intentional fun?
3. James 1:5 says we can ask God for wisdom without worry of rebuke. Spend a few moments praying for your children, and ask God for wisdom on how to win over their hearts even more.

──────────── POWER PRAYER ────────────

Lord, I thank You for giving me _____ to raise. It's an honor to parent and love them in a way that honors You. God, today I'm asking You to enlighten me to areas in which _____ may be struggling. Lord, if there are any words that I am saying or actions that I am committing that are causing pain, guide me away from those. I pray for wisdom on how to navigate these challenges. Show me how I can parent not from my own hurts and insecurities but from Your love. Lord, open my eyes to the giftings You've placed within _____. Teach me how to lead them in the direction You have called them. Lord, I thank You for witty ideas, resources, and strategies to create intentional moments of fun and laughter. Forgive me for allowing

the busyness of life to distract me from simply enjoying _____.
And, Lord, I ask that You help me to be aware of me. Show me how
the pain of my own upbringing or fears are influencing my parenting.
Teach me how to foster the morale of my home so that I may be a
shining light to _____. I worship You and You alone for being
the foundation of my home. May Your love be tangible and set the
tone for every interaction. In Jesus's name. Amen.

Chapter Twelve

UNEXPECTED EXPLOSIONS

My health may fail, and my spirit may grow weak,
but God remains the strength of my heart;
he is mine forever.

PSALM 73:26 NLT

SOME PAIN IS TOO UNBEARABLE to smile through.

In our effort to be good Christians and show our faith, we find ourselves in predicaments where our Sunday-morning church faces are simply masking our inner turmoil. We fake it until we make it while being completely shattered inside. Traumatic moments that we didn't see coming and no one could prepare us for have a tendency to knock the wind out of us. In my own life, during my daughter's seizures and at the passing of my father-in-law, I can remember wondering how I was able to muster up enough strength to breathe amid the debilitating sorrow. We've all faced battles that we didn't see coming—a miscarriage, a death in the family, a disheartening medical diagnosis, a house fire, a divorce, or a car accident that takes a family member, or some other crisis.

The 24-7 job description of a mother magnifies these human struggles. Not only is a mother required to personally heal after crises, but she must also ensure that her children are okay as well. Often our worry for them leaves us even more wounded during these unexpected battles. Sleepless nights, racing thoughts, guilt, and regret overtake us in these hard moments. For most of us, this leads us to wonder . . .

Where were You, God?
Am I not a good Christian?
Am I being punished?
Did God forget about my family?
Why would a God who loves me allow this?

Before long a natural tragedy can become a spiritual tragedy as well. Bitterness toward anyone we think may have been involved and toward God for allowing the situation can consume us. Yet although we will never be able to outrun the struggles of life, we can learn how to cope well and trust God. In the pages that follow, I share the stories of several mothers who remind us that we can be strong and courageous in the midst of perilous times. These stories hold five keys to journeying through the unexpected battles of life: recognizing God's sovereignty, learning to adjust, walking in tenacity, remembering that God is with you, and reaching out for help.

Tammy's Story

The year was 2001. Tammy and her husband, Vandon, had been married for ten years. For Tammy, Vandon was her world and the epitome of what a godly husband should be. He taught his family the Bible and served at church, and together they had a ministry for couples that was blossoming. After being together for over twenty years and having two vibrant boys, ages five and seven, they couldn't wait to bring home their baby girl. In June 2001, when Kaia was born, their family was finally complete. Yet the delivery didn't go as expected. Tammy lost a lot of blood due to a retained placenta, leaving her weak and nearly unable stand or walk afterward. Though this was difficult, with Vandon helping, she knew all would be okay in time.

The day Tammy brought her daughter home, things changed quickly. Hours into Kaia's homecoming, something felt strange. After a long day, Tammy sent her sons upstairs to say good night to their father before she would tuck them in for bed. Yet moments later, her boys seemed unsettled about Vandon, who wouldn't wake up. In a moment of desperation, they called out to their mother. Barely able to walk, Tammy mustered up the little energy she had to walk up the stairs to see what could be wrong with her husband. It was in this moment that she witnessed the worst scene of her life. Vandon was slumped over in an unusual way on his futon. Tammy knew something terrible had happened. To this day, she can't say how she had the strength. All she knew was that her high school sweetheart, her children's father, the man of her dreams, was suddenly gone at the age of thirty-seven of a sudden heart attack—the same day she had brought home their daughter.

With no explanation from God or the medical professionals of how this happened, she found herself a widow, a single mother, and the sole provider for her three children just days after almost losing her own life in childbirth. Before the days of social media campaigns and crowdfunding to raise money, she suddenly had to figure out how she would take care of her family, heal from such a loss, and break the news to her children of the loss of their father. This was the hardest battle of her life. She knew she would have to spend a lifetime helping her children cope with what had occurred. Although the neighborhood, the children's schools, and the church gathered around her, her strength would need to come from the Lord for this battle.

One of the hardest parts about stories like Tammy's is trusting God despite the pain. In my time of knowing Tammy, I've often heard her say that we must trust God's plan. When we choose to trust God's plan, we recognize His sovereignty. According to *Strong's Concordance*, the word *sovereignty* (Greek: *basileia*) means "complete authority and rulership in the world and in the hearts of men."[1] To recognize God's sovereignty is to understand that nothing is allowed without His awareness and to accept this fact. As my grandparents say, "We should have an 'it is well' in our spirits." In other words, no matter what the circumstance, we have to settle within ourselves that if God allowed it, we will be well. Since we will never be able to escape the sufferings of life, our role is to recognize that God always has our best interests at heart and that we must remain steady in our trials. Being a Christian doesn't disqualify us from pain but gives us hope as we experience it. The Bible describes this clearly in the following verses.

> We are hard pressed on every side, but not crushed; perplexed, but not in despair; persecuted, but not abandoned; struck down, but not destroyed. (2 Corinthians 4:8–9)

> Yet what we suffer now is nothing compared to the glory he will reveal to us later. (Romans 8:18 NLT)

> I have told you these things, so that in me you may have peace. In this world you will have trouble. But take heart! I have overcome the world. (John 16:33)

> Consider it pure joy, my brothers, and sisters, whenever you face trials of many kinds, because you know that the testing of your faith produces perseverance. (James 1:2–3)

Hebrews 12:2 (KJV) describes "looking unto Jesus the author and finisher of our faith." In other words, God knows the plans He has for us. I want to spend a few moments leaning into this idea of God being an "author" and a "finisher." As an author, I can personally attest that when it comes to writing a story, I have thought about every detail. Every inflection, every chapter, every character placed within a story is well-thought-out. Nothing is by happenstance or a mistake. In fact, I am well aware of the conclusion and where I want the story to go *before* I ever write a word in a book. If this is the case for me, a human with mere limited capacity and only a few books under my belt, how much more intentional is our God about the story He is writing for us! And He is not just doing this for our story, but for our children's. Each of their stories has been intricately designed to bring God glory; our job is to trust the process. David expressed this same sentiment in the Psalms. He was keenly aware that God was unfolding a glorious story for him before he was even born. "You saw me before I was born. Every day of my life was recorded in your book. Every moment was laid out before a single day had passed" (Psalm 139:16 NLT).

Yes! In our story, there will be plot twists.

Yes! We won't always understand what will happen next.

Yes! We will wonder why certain characters are in our story.

Yes! There may be some unanswered questions.

But I want to draw you back to the word "finisher" in Hebrews 12:2. My friends, God is not a lazy author. As it pertains to you, He didn't just start writing your story and decide to circle back at a later time. Instead, He wrote it and He's finished it. Remember, God does not operate in our time. This is a part of what makes Him such a supreme authority. In Isaiah 46:9–10 (NASB) God said, "I am God . . . declaring the end from the beginning, and from ancient times things which have not been done, saying, 'My plan will be established, and I will accomplish all My good pleasure.'" Yet the harsh truth is that being aware that God knows how the situation will end before it starts can be both frustrating and freeing.

It is up to us to decide whether we will allow tragedies like Tammy's to make us doubt God or run to Him all the more. It's in our brokenness that we can come to recognize the need for God even more. The same God who allowed Vandon to pass away is the same One who had supported Tammy. He was the One who caused people she had never met before to pay her mortgage, help take care of her children, pray for her, and provide meals for her and her children. The same God has used her testimony over and over to steady the hearts of those who've visited her grief support groups. The same God who allowed Tammy's tragedy has also built her strength to endure and to motivate others to do the same even in this exact moment. God not only restored Tammy but showed her children from an early age that their heavenly Father had everything they needed to sustain them. Surely a mother's pain can be used as a time of victory for her children when she embraces the sovereignty of God.

Hagar's Story

Out of all the biblical mothers, Hagar has one of the most unfortunate stories. As a member of the household of Sarai and Abram, she found herself in a predicament where she had no control and would endure much pain. First, I want to give a little of her backstory. In Genesis, God told Abram that he would be the father of many nations. Recognizing that she was much older than childbearing age and still without biological children, Sarai came up with a plan. She would allow her maidservant Hagar and Sarai's husband to sleep together in hopes of producing an heir. (Side note: we cannot cheat our way into God's promises.) Needless to say, Hagar got pregnant. It would seem that what God had spoken earlier was coming to pass. However, this was far from the case. The promised child was to come through Sarai and Abram and not the crafty scheme that had been created.

Once Hagar learned she was pregnant, this naturally caused an issue. As anyone could imagine, living in close quarters with a woman who was now the mother of your husband's child was a recipe for disaster. Before long it was obvious that Hagar and Sarai were frustrated with each other.

> He slept with Hagar, and she conceived.
>
> When she knew she was pregnant, *she began to despise her mistress.* Then Sarai said to Abram, "You are responsible for the wrong I am suffering. I put my slave in your arms, and now that she knows she is pregnant, she despises me. May the LORD judge between you and me."
>
> *"Your slave is in your hands,"* Abram said. "Do with her whatever you think best." *Then Sarai mistreated Hagar*; so she fled from her. (Genesis 16:4–6, emphasis added)

Abram, Sarai, and Hagar each played a role in this scene. Sarai's frustration over being barren and attempting to manipulate God's plan, Abram's choice to go along with it and not take responsibility, and Hagar's choice to dishonor Sarah all caused major turmoil. Yet Hagar and her unborn child would receive the brunt of the situation. Most of us have been in a situation where it wasn't just other people's choices but also our response that caused pain. The hard truth is that many of the unexpected explosions of our lives have been set off by our own actions. Nonetheless, what happened next in Hagar's story is what I want to draw your attention to.

After Hagar ran away into the wilderness, the angel of the Lord appeared to her in her time of desperation. He gave her instructions for what to do next, including returning to Abram and Sarai. God reassured Hagar that a nation would arise from her son and told her to name her son Ishmael (which means "God hears"). Hagar the servant girl went from running from a chaotic situation to standing face-to-face with the Lord. In this moment, He didn't scold her for treating Sarai poorly or shame her for running away. Instead, He spoke life into her and her unborn child. Her response to Him was a key point that we can gather from this tumultuous story. "She gave this name to the LORD who spoke to her: 'You are the God who sees me,' for she said, 'I have now seen the One who sees me'" (Genesis 16:13).

Hagar did something in this moment that no one before her had done—she gave God a personal name: "The God Who Sees Me," or *Beer-lahai-roi* in Hebrew. Take a moment to take that in. In the midst of the worst day of her life, Hagar called God the One who saw her. This moment impacted her so much that she gave God an intimate name that reminded her that He saw past her shame, past her status, past her circumstance and reminded her that He was present for her.

Warrior Mother, there is so much in Hagar's story we can lean into during seasons of brokenness. You see, God didn't just speak into

Hagar's life—He also spoke to her about the life of her unborn child. God not only had a plan to restore Hagar and help her in this situation but also knew what would become of Ishmael before he had breathed his first breath. Hagar's story is a reminder that as mothers, we will find ourselves in situations we didn't expect. Some scenarios will leave us completely broken. Some circumstances will make us want to run away, even when we recognize it may not be an option. There will be times when we feel alone and the Lord is our only support system. Single mothers, military mamas of deployed members, and those who have children with chronic illnesses can relate to this concept more than anyone else.

Yet I want to remind you—you serve the God who sees you! I believe it is no coincidence that this name is the first name we see given to God in the Bible. He wanted us to know up front that His character as a father is one that is intimate and not distant. He doesn't leave us when the situation seems tough, and He's never too far away to answer our call. Moreover, His role as a father in our lives is equally true for our children. Though situations will arise, they have a God who sees them and who knows them. Recognizing this alone will be one of our greatest victories in parenting.

Hagar's story is a reminder that God has a special place in His heart for mothers. In fact, God spoke to several mothers in the Bible who were faced with hard moments. He spoke to Hannah, who was barren, and declared she would give birth. He spoke to Mary, assuring her that He would be with her as she birthed the Messiah. God spoke to Sarai and gave her the promise of a child. I believe God spoke to Jochebed, as she successfully hid Moses from Pharaoh for months, and to Zipporah, who would later save Moses's life after he failed to follow God's command for their son. Yes! God spoke to mothers then and does so even now. Quite simply, God doesn't play around about His children nor the ones taking care of them. He sees us, and He knows what we need. Isaiah 40:11 (NLT) says it beautifully: "He will feed his flock like a shepherd. He will carry the lambs in his arms, holding them close to his heart. He will gently lead the mother sheep with their young."

When the unforeseen explosions of life happen, know that you serve a God who can meet you in your place of shame and sorrow and speak life into you.

I see this verse as one of the greatest promises for mothers everywhere. Our Shepherd carries us close to His heart, and He leads us gently. Our job is to follow His lead and know He is attentive to our circumstances. When the unforeseen explosions of life happen, know that you serve a God who can meet you in your place of shame and sorrow and speak life into you.

Mary's Story

Mary, the mother of Jesus, found herself in an unexpected situation while only a teen. Believed to be twelve to fourteen years old, she was in for quite a surprise when the angel Gabriel visited her and announced that she would carry the Messiah.

> The angel went to her and said, "Greetings, you who are highly favored! The Lord is with you."
> Mary was greatly troubled at his words and wondered what kind of greeting this might be. But the angel said to her, "Do not be afraid, Mary; you have found favor with God. You will conceive and give birth to a son, and you are to call him Jesus. He will be great and will be called the Son of the Most High. The Lord God will give him the throne of his father David, and he will reign over Jacob's descendants forever; his kingdom will never end. (Luke 1:28–33)

Not only was Mary young, not only was she a virgin, not only was she engaged, but she was carrying the Savior of the world. Talk about pressure! From telling her fiancé, Joseph, about the unborn child and the confusion that must have caused, to wondering how she could have what it would take to raise the Son of God, we can assume that Mary felt all the emotions imaginable. Yet her initial response wasn't like what we see with Moses in Exodus, in which he questioned God and wondered how he could be used. Her response wasn't like Sarai's, who laughed when God promised her she would have a son a year later. She didn't even respond like Job and wonder how God could allow certain things to happen that seem irrational. Instead, she said, "'I am the Lord's servant. . . . May your word to me be fulfilled'" (Luke 1:38). I wonder how many women would say "Let it be" when faced with such a situation.

I'm afraid that in hearing the classic Christmas story of the birth of Jesus, we neglect to realize how much Mary had to endure throughout her journey as the mother of Jesus. Truthfully, Gabriel's conversation with Mary was just the beginning. For the biblical prophecies to be fulfilled, Mary's life with Jesus was far from easy. We see this as she traveled over eighty miles to complete the required census late in her pregnancy. This would be where she gave birth to Jesus in a stable, a rather uncomfortable setting for any mother to have a child. Less than two years later, due to King Herod's plot to kill boys under age two, Mary, Joseph, and Jesus found themselves on the run. They would need to quickly leave for Egypt in order to save Jesus's life. God continued to relocate the family by directing Joseph through dreams. They moved back to Israel, then to Judea, and eventually to Nazareth.

Mary's story teaches us one major aspect of journeying through unexpected situations: being willing to adjust. You see, Mary could have complained her entire pregnancy. She could have asked God to explain why they needed to keep moving. She could have asked the Lord to use someone else altogether or even looked into dropping Jesus off at the temple for the priests to raise Him. The stress and pressure of trying to keep Jesus safe while following the lead of her husband, and feeling a sense of ownership over the Savior of the world, could have led her to want to abandon the mission. Yet what we find throughout her story are consistent moments of being willing to adjust to whatever it looked like to be the mother of the Savior. If it meant moving in a split second or calling Him out to do His first miracle or even enduring the agonizing moment of watching Him die on the cross, Mary was all in no matter what. Although her story as a mother had many unsettling moments, she remained faithful to the words spoken to the angel Gabriel, "May your word to me be fulfilled."

I am convinced that one major reason life's circumstances take us out so easily is because we allow ourselves to be rigid in thought and unwilling to accept change. The truth is, some things that God allows are not just because we live in a fallen world but because He wants to build character in us. Unfortunately, we can halt our own and our children's growth by seeing unexpected situations as a stopping point rather than a shifting point. You see, at any point Mary could have refused to follow God's prompting. She could have focused on the irritation of the situation and not the bigness of her God. Yet, as mothers, we must realize that pain can be a sign that a change needs to be made. Rather than run from the pain or allow ourselves to wallow in self-pity, we can ask ourselves some key questions.

- Is God using this situation to shift my thought process?
- Is there anything I could be doing better?
- Is this pain a sign that it's time for me to move on?
- How is my method of processing this situation affecting my child?
- Am I willing to let it be according to God's Word?
- What needs to be adjusted for everyone involved to walk in peace?

These questions may not have easy answers, as they force us to make a self-evaluation. But remember, part of being a champion for our children is to ensure that we are honest with ourselves. Like Mary, we can face unexpected scenarios with an attitude of willingness to follow God's lead. When we surrender our plans completely to Christ, our most unforeseen battles can become our greatest victories.

A Shunammite Woman's Story

Although we may never know her name, the Shunammite woman's story is one in which we can easily see God's hand in the midst of tragedy. Starting in 2 Kings 4:8, she is introduced as a woman who is wealthy, kind, and hospitable. Scripture records her telling her husband about Elisha: "She said to her husband, 'I know that this man who often comes our way is a holy man of God. Let's make a small room on the roof and put in it a bed and a table, a chair and a lamp for him. Then he can stay there whenever he comes to us'" (2 Kings 4:9–10).

This choice to be hospitable granted her great favor, and during a trip to Shunem, Elisha sought to learn how he could bless her in return. Upon talking with his servant, Gehazi, Elisha learned that the Shunammite woman had no children. Elisha leaped at the opportunity to bless her, and after learning this, ensured her, "Next year at this time, you will be holding a son" (4:16). The Shunammite was hesitant about this prophetic word and asked the prophet not to get her hopes up. Yet God delivered on the words of the prophet, and sure enough the Shunammite woman found herself pregnant with a son. It would seem that God blessed her with a gift she hadn't even asked for. This was indeed a victory but just the beginning of her parenting journey.

Unfortunately, the woman's story takes a tragic turn. On a day when he was helping his father, her son had a sudden headache. This pain didn't go away easily, and the Bible says that he died on his mother's lap the same day. Some scholars believe that the quickness of his death signified a brain aneurysm. Yet as unexpected and heartbreaking as this was, what happened next was even more unexpected.

> She went up and laid him on the bed of the man of God, then shut the door and went out.
>
> She called her husband and said, "Please send me one of

the servants and a donkey so I can go to the man of God quickly and return."

"Why go to him today?" he asked. "It's not the New Moon or the Sabbath."

"That's all right," she said.

She saddled the donkey and said to her servant, "Lead on; don't slow down for me unless I tell you." So she set out and came to the man of God at Mount Carmel.

When he saw her in the distance, the man of God said to his servant Gehazi, "Look! There's the Shunammite! Run to meet her and ask her, 'Are you all right? Is your husband all right? Is your child all right?'"

"Everything is all right," she said.

When she reached the man of God at the mountain, she took hold of his feet. Gehazi came over to push her away, but the man of God said, "Leave her alone! She is in bitter distress, but the LORD has hidden it from me and has not told me why."

"Did I ask you for a son, my lord?" she said. "Didn't I tell you, 'Don't raise my hopes'?"

Elisha said to Gehazi, "Tuck your cloak into your belt, take my staff in your hand and run. Don't greet anyone you meet, and if anyone greets you, do not answer. Lay my staff on the boy's face."

But the child's mother said, "As surely as the LORD lives and as you live, I will not leave you." So he got up and followed her. (4:21–30)

Let's take a moment to notice several things the Shunammite woman did here that can help us as we face unexpected battles.

- She didn't announce the death of her son—she simply placed him where she believed he would most likely be healed.
- When her husband attempted to delay her travel, she refused

to wait. She recognized she needed to get to the man of God immediately.

- She didn't use her status as an excuse to send someone else to do the job—she jumped on the donkey herself to travel what some believed was over fifteen miles and what would have taken hours to complete.
- When asked how her son was doing by Gehazi, she said, "Everything is all right." We have to believe this was said from a place of faith, as she was keenly aware that her son had passed away hours before.
- She made a choice to be persistent and insisted that the prophet return to her son with her.

At each of these five crucial moments, we see the Shunammite woman showing clear tenacity. Tenacity is the strong desire to stay attached to an idea or person with a refusal to be torn away. In other words, people who are tenacious reject anything that may separate them from what they feel led to do. We see this quality in the toddler who refuses to be separated from his mother or the teen who insists on doing something she feels she should have the right to do. The Shunammite woman used this fiery passion to see that her son was healed by any means necessary. She used her moments of heartbreak to bring restoration. Her pain was used for a purpose, to bring God glory. Sure enough, God used Elisha to resurrect her son! Her story reminds us of how our persistence during tragedy can be the difference between life and death.

Warrior Mother, we will all face circumstances that will break our hearts. Some situations will be out of our control. But others may require us to dig deep, move aside anyone who is halting the process, and cry out for answers. We hear about this often with mothers who don't stop until they get a second, third, or fourth opinion about their child's ailment. We can also see the tenacity of a mother who is relentless about seeing her child get justice in an unfair situation or more assistance when failing in school. This same tenacity will be what carries the single mother as she balances the loss of her own ideas of what her life would look like with work and caring for a child. Here's what I have learned—no one can *make* you passionate and no one can *take* your passion once you are resolute. Tenacity will carry you through everyday struggles and is the reason wars in the natural and spiritual are won.

Like the Shunammite woman, we have to be willing to advocate and fight, no matter the circumstance. When we lose our inner fight to keep going, the Enemy has us right where he wants us. You see, the Shunammite woman could have chosen to stay in a wounded place. She had just lost her only child, one that God blessed her with when she hadn't even asked for him. Her story could have been one of great weeping and frustration that God would give her a gift and suddenly take it away. Instead, she believed that somehow the Lord would use this for His glory—and He did.

Let us find opportunities to seek God for wisdom in the midst of tragedy, and when He tells us the next step, may we not be so overwhelmed in sorrow that we forget to run with all we have toward His plan. Don't be afraid to fight for it! If God called you to push for it, He will give you the strength. He has the final word. "If you need wisdom, ask our generous God, and he will give it to you. He will not rebuke you for asking" (James 1:5).

Victoria's Story

I leave you with this final story from my own life. In late 2014 I was living what seemed on the surface to be an amazing life. I was a mother of four, and God was elevating me in many areas. In my church, I led in worship, was the middle school coordinator, and worked closely with my husband to help with the volunteer ministry. Outside of church, I was the assistant director for the local MOPS (Mothers of Preschoolers) group, and I hosted my own Bible study, Armed for Battle, for military women. I even had a side job as a Disney vacation specialist, and my services were becoming the most talked about in town.

On the outside, I was excelling in every area, and God's hand was all over my life. Yet on the inside, I was hurting tremendously. Motherhood was kicking my butt, my marriage was failing, I felt overworked and underappreciated at church, and the other ministries I led were more strenuous than I had imagined. As each day passed, it felt as though a dark cloud was hovering over me. In public I had mastered the fake smile and bubbly personality to mask my pain, but at home I was in a deep depression, hardly able to get out of bed, angry with everyone, and full of tears. This lasted for months, and I prayed someone would notice. I felt as though I was sinking . . . literally.

One day while in the bath, I thought, *What if I just sink? What if I just sink and not come up?* I imagined how I could take pills if that didn't work or what options would make it seem like an accident. I could hear tormenting whispers of how the world would be so much better without me. If I were to die, I could be free from the pressure of needing to be perfect and "doing all the things." A few minutes after processing these thoughts, I decided to keep fighting another day. After all, who would fulfill my roles? I am sad to say that the only reason I didn't follow through with my suicidal thought that day was because I knew I had places to show up to the next day that needed my help. At that point, I was living only to show up for everyone else and never myself or the Lord. Sadly, I know I'm not alone.

A couple days after this bath-time experience, my mind kept flashing back to just . . . sinking . . . in. I regretted not just going under. A few days later, my husband and I were scheduled to go to a leadership meeting. All day long it was as though nothing in me wanted to enter that door. My stomach turned all day, and I was physically ill throughout the meeting. The whole day I struggled between wanting to attend in hopes of receiving prayer but also terrified that my deep depression would be outed in front of everyone. If we're honest, any sign of mental weakness can be greeted with disdain in many churches.

As to be expected, within five minutes of entering the meeting, the pastor of the church said, "Victoria, we need to pray for you right now. I'm not quite sure why yet. But stand in the middle." My deer-in-the-headlights look was the understatement of the year. Over twenty-five leaders gathered around me in a circle and took turns praying and prophesying over me. It felt as if people were pulling layers of old dusty coats off my back. With each word, I felt lighter. Each word, each prayer, pierced my heart. Each word affirmed that my motherhood was intentional and that God had a plan for me. Each word was spoken in love, grace, and truth. No one judged and no one condemned. I was surrounded by God's amazing love through His people. By the time I left the room, my cloud of sorrow had been replaced with unspeakable joy. I was a different person. I am so thankful to say that I've never experienced another suicidal thought. Although I didn't solicit the prayer, I have no doubt that the prayers that day are the reason I am here today.

Don't experience life's battles alone. Oftentimes we shy away from help because, as mothers, we are supposed to be the strong ones. Yet every single story I have shared, from Tammy's story to my own, show mothers who didn't journey through tough times alone. I'm convinced that isolation is the key way the Enemy can attack you. Remember, no war is won alone. It is through connecting with others that we can be vulnerable, share resources, and learn that we are not alone. Trust me— heartbreak hits differently when you don't have the support needed to carry you through. Find others who can pray for you and meet you with grace when you journey through tough times. Mothers are not immune to heartache, but together we can find home in one another's stories of triumph. We will talk about this more in the next chapter.

Purpose in the Pain

Long ago I learned to stop asking God why. When unexpected tragedy happens, we typically want answers. If it involves our children, we really take it to heart and wonder why God would allow it. The truth is, we may never get those answers. But what if instead of asking God *why* things happened or *when* things will get better, we ask Him *how* the tragedy can be used for His glory and *what* He wants us to learn?

Is there a ministry to be discovered?

Is God calling me to shift?

How can I use this crisis to know God better?

How can this situation build my faith?

What would you have me to do next, Lord?

In answering these questions, we will see God reveal His marvelous plans for us.

I leave you with the words of my grandfather Bishop Eddie L. Stevens, who has been preaching and teaching the gospel for sixty-plus years: "Everyone will face the hard times in life. Some people just have no God to call on when they do."

Warrior Mother, you have a God to call on when you face tough circumstances. One of our greatest victories as Christians is that we have a God who is *alive*! He is not in a statue or buried in a grave. Yes, we will face heartaches, some indescribable. But we have a God who is accessible at all times. He will give us the strength we need and the courage to go forward despite the obstacles.

May we trust in God's sovereignty like Tammy.

Know that we aren't alone like Hagar.

Be willing to adjust our thoughts and actions to His will like Mary.

Walk in tenacity like the Shunammite woman.

Receive help like Victoria.

Walk in faith that God will bring strategy and healing, like a champion fully reliant on Him.

VICTORY VERSE

The LORD is near to the brokenhearted and saves those who are crushed in spirit. (Psalm 34:18 NASB)

REFLECTIONS

1. Which story reminded you the most of something you have been through or are currently experiencing? What has God taught you in these moments?

2. What tragedies in your life have you seen God use as a way to minister to others?

3. Read James 1:2–5. How has this unfolded in your life? Write a prayer for what you would say to another mother experiencing heartache, using the concepts of James 1:2–5.

———————————— POWER PRAYER ————————————

Lord, I thank You that You are near the brokenhearted. Nothing catches You off guard. Although there will be hard moments, I can rejoice, for You never leave me. Your Word says that You are near those who take care of the young, and I thank You for that. There are days when I need You more than ever. There are moments when I don't know how I can go on without Your help. Yet in every circumstance, You are there. God, I ask that You help me to accept that You are the author of my story. Help me to embrace this and learn to adjust without complaint. Take the lead in my life and my motherhood. Show me how to be an example of journeying through pain and staying in faith. In Jesus's name. Amen.

Chapter Thirteen

BATTLE BUDDIES

You cannot fight and win a battle alone.
PASTOR JOSEPH RIOLLANO

WE WERE MEANT TO DO life together.

Although the world seems more connected, we are more distant than ever. It wasn't always this way. I hold dear memories of life before social media and cell phones. After a busy day at school or work, I would race into my home and go straight to the house phone. I knew every friend's number by heart and couldn't wait to tell them about my day. Three-way phone calls kept us all in the loop, and for those who were really advanced, an email chain could lead to some truly fun conversations. In other words, having deep friendships required great intention. There was no looking online for an update if your friend had her baby or you learned of a tragedy. Quite frankly, if you didn't pick up the phone and make a choice to be present, you would have no idea what was happening in another person's life. Friends were made and kept through action.

Even Jesus had friends during His time on earth. He chose to live deeply with them. His disciples were not just trainees who needed to follow orders. Instead, He never found Himself too occupied to eat with them, commune with them, and encourage them. He would ask these same friends to pray with Him in His toughest moments.

Warrior Mother, you cannot battle alone. From the beginning of time, we see that man was made for community. Just as it was not good for Adam to be alone in the garden, the same is true for you today. One of the Enemy's attack strategies is to keep us isolated. If you've found yourself purposely avoiding close friends, making excuses not to leave your home, and refusing to reach out to others when you're in need, you may be struggling with isolation. The Bible says it like this: "Two people are better off than one, for they can help each other succeed. If one person falls, the other can reach out and help. But someone who falls alone is in real trouble" (Ecclesiastes 4:9–10 NLT).

We all need a battle buddy. Someone who can lift us up in the midst of intense struggle and someone who can rejoice with us in our greatest triumph. As a military spouse, this concept of having a battle buddy is one I hear often. When speaking to members of the military community, I hear of men who have formed deep bonds with other men. These are people they've trained with, fought in battles alongside, celebrated promotions with, and grieved with. There's something about learning alongside one another and having one another's backs during the unthinkable that creates lifetime friendships. Even hospitals have begun to recognize the importance of camaraderie, instituting battle-buddy systems. Some hospitals match the practitioners and nurses with other medical professionals for peer support. In other medical facilities, military veterans are matched with current soldiers to help them recognize that they can be resilient in the toughest battles, from the loss of limbs to feeling suicidal.[1]

We need one another. When one is weak, the other is strong. When one needs encouragement, the other may offer uplifting words that soothe the soul. I believe the reason so many mothers struggle is because they are attempting to raise children while feeling completely alone. Perhaps you can relate to feeling like the emotional safe space for so many others but having no one to call on for yourself. As a pastor's wife, this has been my own testimony for years. Carrying the weight of life plus being responsible for other little people's well-being is a heavy load to take on, and it can lead to depression. This is why the Word says we are to "carry each other's burdens, and in this way you will fulfill the law of Christ" (Galatians 6:2). Sometimes we operate under the false pretense that we can just handle everything on our own. A little prayer and a visit to church will help us conquer life's issues. But in reality, that isn't enough.

The story of Naomi and Ruth gives us a powerful example of battle buddies. In the book of Ruth, we find Naomi, an older woman whose husband and two adult sons had died. At this juncture, her two daughters-in-law were with her still, all suffering from the immense loss. Naomi, in an act of kindness, implored the two daughters-in-law, one being Ruth, to each return to her own mother and find a new husband. It would seem the most advantageous plan for Ruth to start her life over again. Yet listen to what Ruth said in this crucial moment: "Don't urge me to leave you or to turn back from you. Where you go I will go, and where you stay I will stay. Your people will be my people and your God my God. Where you die I will die, and there I will be buried. May the LORD deal with me, be it ever so severely, if even death separates you and me" (Ruth 1:16–17).

This is a picture of true friendship. A friend is one who makes a choice to journey alongside you even when times are difficult. One who stays with you when everyone else leaves. One who prays with you and believes the best for you. Ruth and Naomi's friendship wasn't affected by age or status. They made a choice to remain connected with each other, no matter the circumstance. Ruth's decision to be loyal to Naomi continues throughout the book, as she eventually worked to support them both. Naomi returned the favor by being a source of wisdom as Ruth entered into a relationship with Boaz. Amazingly, Boaz and Ruth's line would later produce King David and eventually Jesus. Ruth's act of friendship was not only beneficial to her but would put her in the prime position to bless many.

Ruth and Naomi are the perfect example that friendship can be a beautiful blessing for everyone involved. We were never meant to face life's struggles alone. We were never meant to answer hard topics alone. We were never even meant to parent alone. The basic design for procreation proves this inherently. Yet we find ourselves taking on the weight of parenting in a bubble. I've found myself crying out, wishing I had another mom who understood my frustrations. I've wondered who I could call that wouldn't judge me for having a bad parenting day. I've prayed for years for God to send me a tribe of women I can glean from and be an inspiration to. So from personal experience, I can attest that the worst place for a mother to be is *alone*!

In this chapter, I will teach you how you can find battle buddies in your parenting journey. Having someone alongside you who can encourage you not to give up when battles come will be a major part of your success in parenting.

A Battle Buddy Should Be Mission Minded

As Christian mothers, we must remember our ultimate mission: to draw our children closer to the Lord and teach them how to resist every attack of the Enemy. We must reach a point in our maturity where we refuse to allow anyone not focused on this mission within our close circle. This doesn't mean we push away anyone who isn't spiritually mature. It does mean that when it comes to being vulnerable or needing someone to pray for us, we can easily discern who to call and who not to call. One mistake we often make as women is to look for buddies who are in a similar life stage and lifestyle or with families that match ours in size. But this is not always the best-case scenario. I have found time and time again that your vision for parenting doesn't have to be the same, but your missions must align.

Let me explain. Every person has a vision of what it looks like to parent a child. Consider the following example. Suppose your neighbor has a strong conviction about healthy living. She feeds her children organic food, and no junk food is allowed. They are on a strict schedule of when and how to eat to achieve the highest health goals. You, on the other hand, have no issue with eating out a couple times a week and rewarding well-behaved children with candy. In this case, your vision and your neighbor's vision of parenting are not aligned.

However, this same neighbor fiercely loves the Lord. She has shown up for your family when you had a child by providing an amazing salad and homemade chili made from the healthiest organic products. This same neighbor will gladly grab your child from the bus and pray for you when you are in a bind. Moreover, she is training her children to know and love the Lord. With every conversation you have with her, you're stronger as a person. In this case, your vison of day-to-day parenting is different. But your mission is the same! This is a recipe for victory. As long as there is a mutual respect where the differences arise, you can be assured that God can bless your friendship, and you may even learn from one another.

The issue is that we also try to create cookie-cutter friendships. Before we are willing to attempt a friendship, we assess how many kids the family has, what church they go to, and whether her husband and yours will get along. We try to find a friend whose life is like ours on the outside rather than looking at inside matters. My own past friendships that were the least successful were the ones that appeared to be a perfect match. I went into these friendships with an expectation that the other person's life would be just like mine. Let's just say we both ended up disappointed. We cannot automatically dismiss potential friendships or even assume that some will qualify based on outside demographics alone. Just as the Lord looks at the heart, we must be careful to find people who are *searching* for God and not just those who may fill a void for us. Instead of trying to find mothers who parent the same, seek to find those who love the Lord with the same fervor as you do.

A Battle Buddy Should Be Available

When considering who God has called you to run alongside, you must take a practical look at who's available. Again, looks can be deceiving. In my own life, I have had many people who heard of my family size or role in our church and assumed I was unavailable. Little did they know my days tend to be flexible and I work from home. Their assumption that I was too busy wasn't a true one and kept them from reaching out in a time of need. I encourage you to test the waters with this. Ask yourself these questions:

- Who responds when I call?
- Who follows up with me when they haven't seen me in a while?
- Who offers to hang out with me?
- Who invites me over?
- Who accepts my invitation?
- Who offers to help?
- Who reaches out to me for no reason at all but to say hello?
- Who shows up?

The answers to these questions will alert you to who is available. Sometimes we want a friendship so badly that we ignore the obvious signs that the person is too busy, uninterested in a deeper friendship, or is attempting to put distance between the two of you. Now, it is true there are some friendships that can naturally pick up after months or even years of not seeing or talking to each other. These childhood or college friendships are not the ones I am addressing. Rather, the goal is to find true battle buddies that you can journey through motherhood together with.

Availability doesn't mean the person always has to be accessible to you. (We will address boundaries a bit later.) It does mean that the person shows the common courtesy of answering a call or text, or even checks on you in a time of need. And when she cannot respond, she at least follows up with a genuine concern for you to ensure all is well.

An available friend is one who doesn't see your friendship as a burden or business transaction in which you each only reach out for personal needs. Instead, one who is available is one who desires to be present in your life in person or over the phone and in action. For anyone to qualify for your inner circle, she must make a choice to devote time to you, simply because. If you're the only one reaching out, the only one calling, the only one showing up, it's possible that it's time to reevaluate the deepness of the friendship and respond accordingly.

A Battle Buddy Should Be Honest

We must find honest friends. Our tendency is to find friends who validate our opinions, poor choices, and lifestyles. Surrounding ourselves with people who affirm our beliefs is called "confirmation bias." It's one way to quickly fall into deception and never allow God to renew flawed thinking. This is far from what the Lord has called us to do. Instead, He calls us to find friends who will strengthen us and, at times, bring conviction. When both friends are open to correction and vulnerable, this can be a beautiful thing. The key is to find a person who can balance grace and truth. Grace is the ability to be kind, even when you feel that it is undeserved. Truth would be defined as sharing what is accurate, genuine, and correct. In our case, truth would be anything that points us back to the Word of God. Whatever the case may be, we must balance the truth with grace. Too much of one and not enough of another will always be problematic. Here's what the Lord has shown me: Too much truth without grace makes you a blunt and rude person. Too much grace without truth makes you an enabler.

> He calls us to find friends who will strengthen us and, at times, bring conviction.

If you operate as a person who shares a lot of truth without grace, you will warrant little respect. Those who act this way are known for having no filter. This kind of person never makes an ideal battle buddy. The words she says will pierce both you and your child, and you will be unable to keep up with the hurl of insults and demeaning moments. Before long your battle buddy will be the one inflicting most of your wounds. Whether she is telling you the truth of the Word in a way that uses Scripture to demean or make you feel like a worthless parent, or she is sharing the "truth" of her opinion with unsolicited advice, be careful with those who cannot tame their tongues. I love the way the Word speaks of the power of the tongue: "The tongue can bring death or life; those who love to talk will reap the consequences" (Proverbs 18:21 NLT).

Can you be friends with a person with a sharp tongue? Sure! Should you share your inner secrets with that person? No! We have enough battles to deal with when it comes to fighting our own flesh and the attacks of the Enemy. Let us not allow ourselves to receive friend-inflicted wounds that aren't so easily healed.

Friends who are high on grace and low on truth are just as detrimental to your mental state. These friends will listen to you share about how you mistreated your husband or children and not say a word—not that they should judge or treat you poorly if you share something unsettling. However, I want to draw us to the verse that's often shared when discussing friendships: "As iron sharpens iron, so a friend sharpens a friend" (Proverbs 27:17 NLT).

According to Matthew Poole's commentary, iron sharpening iron is a powerful concept because, in many ways, the symbol of one sword or knife being rubbed against another signifies that both blades will be made into their most effective shapes. When a man spends time with another, he is "greatly refreshed, his very wits are sharpened, and his spirit revived, and he is both fitted for and provoked to action."[2] Warrior Mother, finding a friend who is willing to have a moment of tension with you to see you win in life may be the best thing that ever happens to you. If you genuinely want a person who can be a strong support system, ask the Lord to send you a friend who can be truthful in such a way that brings restoration, not condemnation. As a bonus, be sure to pray that you can be the same for someone else. A healthy balance of grace + truth = life-giving conversations. "Better is open rebuke than hidden love. Wounds from a friend can be trusted, but an enemy multiplies kisses" (Proverbs 27:5–6).

A Battle Buddy Should Have a Servant's Heart

Those who battle alongside you in life should have a heart to serve and give. Oftentimes friendships become one-sided, where one is the primary consumer. One friend will serve the other by reaching out, showing up, praying, and helping with practical needs. The other will tend to receive the benefit of the friendship and make little effort.

This is not what true friendship looks like. Can you imagine what this would look like on a literal battlefield? In my mind, I can envision two soldiers heading off into battle. While one is working hard to spot the Enemy, being aware of the potential traps, holding on to his fifty-pound rucksack, and carrying out the mission of the commander, the other is simply sitting on the sidelines watching it unfold. Instead of giving a hand and being active in battle, the lackluster friend would just sit back, possibly barking out requests the entire time. The battle buddy who should be active in battle would be complaining, "Hey, friend, can you carry my rucksack too?" "Hey, friend, I know you're busy, but I was wondering if I could borrow your helmet?" This self-centered friend would be more of a liability than an asset.

When we're searching for those to be in our inner circle, we must ask ourselves who among us has a servant's heart. A friend with this kind of heart is always asking, "How can I help?" They are quick to recognize when something isn't quite right about you or when you need emotional support. We see the actions that come from having a servant's heart in our Savior. He had every right to demand that the disciples do a list of things for Him. He easily could have used His friends to serve His every emotional or physical need—after all, He was royalty. Yet this is not the picture we see as Jesus washed the feet of the disciples.

When he had finished washing their feet, he put on his clothes and returned to his place. "Do you understand what I have done for you?" he asked them. "You call me 'Teacher' and 'Lord,' and rightly so, for that is what I am. Now that I, your Lord and Teacher, have washed your feet, you also should wash one another's feet. I have set you an example that you should do as I have done for you. Very truly I tell you, no servant is greater than his master, nor is a messenger greater than the one who sent him. Now that you know these things, you will be blessed if you do them." (John 13:12–17)

In this act of humility, Jesus did the work that should have been assigned to the lowest of servants. Although the disciples didn't understand why Jesus would desire to serve them, Jesus used this as a teaching moment. True friendship and love are modeled best when we serve one another. In so many words, Jesus was saying, "If you really want to be blessed, be willing to do the dirty work and serve others through action." If you're too proud, arrogant, or busy, or believe your social status is too high to serve another person, how can you display God's heart? This concept isn't just for our friendships but even our parenting! We are called to see serving one another and our children as a privilege, not a burden. If your friendships are based only around what you can get from the other person, or those in your close circle spend most of their time draining from you and never giving, this is a problem.

A Battle Buddy Should Be Prayerful

Our battle buddies must be people of genuine prayer. Although this may seem like a given, our friendships should never be so imbalanced that we are the only ones praying. I have seen far too often that friends we had before getting serious about the Lord will remain in a high place with us. On one hand, this is an amazing asset. Certainly Jesus was far more spiritually sound than those He called friends. So much so that many questioned how He could spend time with sinners and those deemed unworthy. Yet if we look at the Gospel accounts, we see that Jesus's disciples were young men who were hungry to know more. They asked Jesus how to pray. They learned how to do miracles and cast out demons. So although the disciples could never rise to be Jesus's equal spiritually, they sure were zealous to learn all they could. These are the types of people you need in your corner.

One of my best friends happens to be a woman thirty years older than me. What I love about her is not the fact that we can talk about politics, our different opinions, or racism for hours, but that she is willing to stop everything to pray for me. I cannot count how many times she's sent me a prayer via text message at just the right time.

Her words are always exactly what I need to carry me through the day. I am certain this is because she is always praying for me. What a blessing to know that when I am at my weakest moments, I have a person covering me in prayer.

A friend who wars with you in prayer is like having a personal shield bearer. You can count on this person to have your back when you're feeling overwhelmed with life's battles and know that when you feel like you can no longer fight, she can step in and intercede on your behalf! When you've run out of tears and words to say, she can lift you up with a word of encouragement and by speaking the Word of the Lord over your circumstance. So although your unsaved friends from middle school may offer some amazing advice, they can only take you so far. And when it comes to spiritual matters, you can be assured that they won't be a valuable resource to you.

A Battle Buddy Should Be Good Company

The final aspect of finding a strong friend is to seek those who are a positive influence. The Bible makes it clear: "Do not be deceived: 'Bad company corrupts good morals'" (1 Corinthians 15:33 NASB). We simply cannot outrun the fact that those we allow in our lives will have either a positive or negative effect on us. Sadly, we can expect that those we bring close to us will also impact our parenting and how we view everyday circumstances. If you have a friend who's extraordinarily negative, before long you will find yourself being critical. If your best friend drinks until she passes out, tells everyone's business, or curses like a sailor, your children will eventually be exposed to her behavior. Even if you never commit such acts, they will equate the behavior as being acceptable because you allow it in your presence.

If you find that you often have to explain or justify the actions of your close friends, it may be time for you to pray about your relationships. Again, Jesus spent time with people whom many may have shunned. Our goal shouldn't be to disregard or push away those who aren't perfect examples of Christianity. However, if those in your close circle are leading you away from Christ and not toward Him, these friends are not eligible to be your battle buddies. Those running alongside us in parenting should have the heart of Jesus Christ in private and in public. The Word of God makes it clear that we simply cannot overlook the lifestyle choices that reflect darkness in the following verses:

Have nothing to do with the fruitless deeds of darkness, but rather expose them. (Ephesians 5:11)

Do not make friends with a hot-tempered person, do not associate with one easily angered, or you may learn their ways and get yourself ensnared. (Proverbs 22:24–25)

Do not be yoked together with unbelievers. For what do righteousness and wickedness have in common? Or what fellowship can light have with darkness? (2 Corinthians 6:14)

When you follow the desires of your sinful nature, the results are very clear: sexual immorality, impurity, lustful pleasures, idolatry, sorcery, hostility, quarreling, jealousy, outbursts of anger, selfish ambition, dissension, division, envy, drunkenness, wild parties, and other sins like these. Let me tell you again, as I have before, that anyone living that sort of life will not inherit the Kingdom of God. (Galatians 5:19–2 NLT)

Although it may feel harsh, the most loving thing we can do for ourselves and our children is to place them around others who have a lifestyle that honors the Lord. As heartbreaking as it may be, it would be better to shift a relationship now that is causing pain than to allow it to destroy your home in the long run. The choice to do so reflects that your children outweigh every friendship. Even more so, aligning yourself with those who reflect the truth of God's Word gives your children the opportunity to gain a community of Christian mothers they can run to in a time of need.

My prayer is that you can see the importance of finding fellow mothers who can be a source of strength for you. Imagine the beauty of two or more women coming together on a mission to see God radically move in their lives and in their children's lives. Consider the victories that can be won over an encouraging text message or a time of in-person prayer. One of the best gifts we can give ourselves is to let down our walls and seek God-fearing friends. I am convinced that if you show up and be the friend that you desire others to be toward you, God will certainly bring the battle buddies you need in this time of your life.

Be prayerful.

Be a good friend.

Don't battle alone.

VICTORY VERSE

Though one may be overpowered, two can defend themselves. A cord of three strands is not quickly broken. (Ecclesiastes 4:12)

REFLECTIONS

1. Who would you consider your battle buddy? What makes this relationship different?
2. How have you seen your friendships impact your children? (Positively or negatively)
3. What area of friendship do you feel you can improve in (mission-mindedness, availability, honesty, prayerfulness, good company)? What is one tangible step you can take toward this today?

POWER PRAYER

Lord Jesus, I praise You for the revelation I have received about friendships. Father, I am asking You today to send strong women into my life. Send those I can journey alongside in everyday life and in battle. Show me who I can count on that I may have overlooked. Lord, forgive me if I have misjudged people or pushed away those You have attempted to bring into my life. God, I ask that You help me to be a good friend. May those who call me friend see me as an asset, not a liability. Show me, Lord, the friends I need in my life and my child's life. God, give me the grace and wisdom to pivot, change, or remove relationships that do not honor You. I surrender this area to You. May I be guided by Your wisdom and not my own emotion. I trust You, Lord. In Jesus's name. Amen.

Chapter Fourteen

THE POWER OF REGROUPING

We are never defeated unless we give up on God.
RONALD REAGAN

YEARS BEFORE WE HAD OUR first child, my husband and I uttered
the phrase every nonparent says: "Our children will never . . ." The
parentless version of ourselves believed our kids would never jump
on couches, talk back, tell lies, or say phrases without the southern
charm of "Yes, ma'am" or "No, ma'am." We quickly learned that
these expectations were far from the truth. With over eighteen years
of childcare experience, an associate degree in teacher's education,
and a bachelor's degree in child development between us at the time,
we discovered by our second child that we were out of our league.
Instead of snuggling up to watch romantic movies at night, we spent
our evenings taking notes from *Supernanny* on how to get control of
our rowdy bunch.

You may relate to the struggle between expectation and reality
when it comes to parenting. Although we imagine what our children will look and act like, emotional battles, behavioral concerns,
imperfect health, and spiritual differences are inevitable. Even the
best-behaved child will face a struggle that he or she will be unprepared for. Whether you have a child who is sneaky, has a hard time
reading, or is defiant, as a mother you must come to understand that
your children are growing and learning lessons as they go. In fact,

I'll often look at one of my children and remind myself that this little person has only been alive for a handful of years.

The three-year-old who has a tantrum over being denied another piece of candy does not understand the pain of cavities or relate to the cost of dental care.

The eight-year-old who struggles to read and refuses to try can't comprehend how being an illiterate adult will hinder him in his future career.

The teen who believes her parent is unfair for restricting her social media fails to realize the danger of child trafficking or the emotional repercussions of internet bullying.

The unmarried young adult who continually has unprotected sex may have seen others experience unwanted pregnancy but be unaware of the heavy weight of parenting and the financial ramifications.

In other words, when we make a choice to stop and conceptualize the ages of our children and their lack of experience in many situations, we can stand in a place of grace. Remember, unwanted behaviors are a symptom of a lack of understanding or care for the consequences.

Our choices and rationalizations are based on the awareness and acceptance of the implications. When we fail to fully understand the implications, we will continually make flawed, uninformed decisions. When we consider the behaviors of our children, we must realize that (in most cases) it's the lack of understanding we are battling more than the behavior itself. Truthfully, our children's version of what is right and acceptable may not match up to ours for years to come. This knowledge empowers us to give grace to our children, as we are reminded that we, too, in comparison to an all-knowing God, understand little and fall into error daily. Our responsibility shifts from simply praying for the behavior to stop to praying that God would open the eyes of their hearts to understand the consequences of their actions and give them strategies to do the right things. "A youngster's heart is filled with foolishness" (Proverbs 22:15 NLT), so children need God's guidance just as adults do.

Our job as mothers is to display God's love, mercy, and grace as our children grow into a place of understanding. In times when correction is needed, we must remember to whom they belong. As we seek the Lord, we can ask Him for wisdom on how to navigate each issue we encounter with His children. There will never be a perfect child, but there will always be an all-knowing God who knows what's best for him or her.

An Imperfect Duo

Although many can accept that there's no such thing as a blameless child, as mothers we tend to expect perfection from ourselves. Just as we imagine what our children will be like before they are born, we also envision ourselves as mothers. In a society driven by media, we often are fed an unfair picture of reality. From the perfectly planned gender reveals to the well-polished family photos, motherhood is made to look glamorous. Yet what happens to the mother who is faced with postpartum depression, a sickly child, or the sudden awareness that her child has been abused? What happens to the mother whose children are ungrateful or difficult, or who refuse to believe the gospel? In most cases, these mothers are left riddled with shame and eventually resort to isolation.

Many mothers cannot relate to being a warrior. In fact, daily situations and unexpected explosions may lead you to wonder how you could ever be victorious. I've had times when I cried more than I laughed and screamed more than I hugged. I carried an immense amount of shame that I couldn't live up to the facade I'd created. My own insecurities and guilt from not being the perfect parent left me wounded in many ways. Each day I dreaded getting out of bed to face another day of the parenting battle. Leading my little children well was a fleeting thought as I was trying to survive the war within my own mind. Interestingly, these moments happened just as much when I was a mother of one as they did when I became a mother of seven. The number of children was never what strengthened my mental state. I was imperfect and my children were imperfect—an imperfect duo. What made a difference was my ability to seek the Lord in all things and to reach out for help when I no longer possessed the coping skills to carry on.

A Look at Eve

In the Bible, we discover that many mothers found themselves in painful situations that left them with much guilt. Eve, the first woman, wife, and mother, was not exempt. Regardless of whether you blame Adam or Eve for the first sin, one cannot deny the influence Eve had in this crucial moment in human history. With a single bite of the forbidden fruit, the world was catapulted into a never-ending cycle of sin and shame. Yet readers of Eve's story often focus on the initial poor choice but neglect to consider the many resulting repercussions.

> When the woman saw that the fruit of the tree was good for food and pleasing to the eye, and also desirable for gaining wisdom, she took some and ate it. She also gave some to her husband, who was with her, and he ate it. Then the eyes of both of them were opened, and they realized they were naked; so they sewed fig leaves together and made coverings for themselves. (Genesis 3:6–7)

To truly understand the intensity of Eve's imperfect situation, it is helpful to consider the field of crisis counseling. In his book *Crisis Counseling: A Guide for Pastors and Professionals*, Scott Floyd focuses on the differences between loss, trauma, and crises. He defines loss as the removal of something important, trauma as a sudden disturbing change, and crisis as a problematic state of being that can affect many.[1]

When we look at the life of Eve, the eating of the fruit was only the beginning of what she would experience. The introduction of sin into the world created a chain reaction of loss, trauma, and crises. Eve would lose her place of residence in the garden, her ability to walk without shame, and eventually her second child. She would also experience the trauma associated with losing her life of perfection, having her husband blame her in front of God, and eventually learning that one of her children had murdered another. Lastly, Eve's world was in a complete crisis after she ate the fruit. She was now adjusting to a world where sin was prevalent, dwelling with a husband who had to work tirelessly for food that once came freely, and facing the reality of her own eventual death. To make matters worse, she knew well that her choice was a central part of all the calamity. In the world of counseling, Eve had enough issues at hand to warrant years' worth of sessions.

I interact with many mothers who find themselves in similar situations. When they look back over their lives and parenting journeys, they can see how their choices impacted their children. Whether they learn that their children have experienced abuse at the hand of a family friend or the family unit has become separated through divorce, many mothers come to realize they are unable to create the perfect childhood experience they had imagined. The guilt of not having all the answers or not being able to save children from the schemes of the Enemy can lead mothers to feel like failures. It is inevitable that we will make a choice that causes harm, shows favoritism toward a child, leads to being too tough on another, prevents us from offering forgiveness, and promotes saying things that lead to a lifetime of pain. As explained earlier, not only are we parenting imperfect children, but we are also imperfect ourselves. Without God in our corner, this is a recipe for disaster. Yet we must come to understand that much like the child who doesn't understand the ramifications of his actions, we will say and do things that require daily grace from our Father in heaven.

Making a mistake as a parent is not the ultimate tragedy. In fact, the biggest defeat is when we allow ourselves to believe we are failures and begin to internalize guilt. It's in the place of shame and guilt that the Enemy can spread venomous lies about who we are as mothers. When we start to internalize guilt, it affects every area of our lives. Those who struggle with guilt may experience these symptoms:

- Physically—stomach pain, trouble sleeping, tearfulness
- Mentally—anxiety, obsessive compulsive disorder, lower self-esteem, survivor's guilt, depression
- Interpersonally—overcompensating, paranoia in relationships, isolation

Guilt is a heavy emotion to carry—literally. A study by Princeton University polled a group of people and asked them to rank how often they feel guilty. Afterward these individuals were asked to share how much they believed they physically weighed. The study found that people who reported struggling with guilt also reported themselves as being much heavier in weight than they really were. However, those who scored lesser feelings of guilt and shame tended to guess their weights almost exactly. Additionally, when participants were asked to speak on unethical decisions, most would moments later report their weights as feeling heavier. Guilt was not just a fleeting emotion but one that could be felt in a tangible sense.[2]

In many ways, carrying guilt is comparable to carrying a heavy load on one's back. As a military spouse, I can recall seeing my husband's rucksack for the first time after he returned from boot camp. I was astonished as he pulled what seemed like his entire life out of the bag. Not only was he trained to walk for miles with almost one hundred pounds on his back, but he was also told it was necessary for survival as a military member. Within this bag, communication devices, first aid kits, extra clothes, food, and ammunition may be carried to the battlefield. For a soldier, a rucksack is needed to carry the tools for effective warfare.

The weight of guilt operates in the opposite manner of the military rucksack. Instead of being a supply bag of resources, guilt leaves us with baggage that leads to our own self-sabotage. Instead of having a bag that delivers hope, we will have one that carries trauma, depression, paranoia, or fear over every choice. The mother who should be a champion for her children becomes a weighed-down warrior unable to face herself in the mirror, much less stand against the Enemy.

She finds herself at war with her own self. In Psalm 13:2 we see that this struggle is not new to humankind: "How long must I wrestle with my thoughts and day after day have sorrow in my heart? How long will my enemy triumph over me?" The war against one's own mind is often most difficult to resolve. This internal struggle can either halt us or empower us to regroup and try something new—the choice is ours.

The Power to Regroup

Many mental health professionals believe that the initial onset of guilt can be productive. Guilt can highlight the need for a change of behavior and can drive empathy and better choices in the future. For instance, suppose a parent discovers her child has several cavities. The initial guilt of giving the child too many sweets or not making him floss can be used to encourage better dental hygiene in the future. In a more serious scenario, the mother whose child gets into fights at school may recognize the need for a more disciplined home. When negative situations arise, we can choose to wallow in self-pity or reevaluate how things can be done differently and with greater emphasis on building up the child rather than on the child living in defeat. As long as we choose to stay in pity, we will never walk in peace.

In war, creating new strategies for victory is not a new phenomenon. One can easily see how failure in battle prompted new weaponry to be created and new tactics to be enacted. One of the most intriguing examples of regrouping occurred in the Battle of Pelusium during the Persian War of 525 between Persia and Egypt. In this battle, the Persian army learned of their opponent's deep reverence for cats. Rather than relying on their normal tactics, shields, armor bearers, and swords, they made a choice to re-strategize how war was done. In a clever move, the Persians released more than five hundred cats ahead of them on the battlefield and painted the image of an Egyptian goddess on their shields and helmets. The thought of injuring a cat or one they saw as a god created pandemonium for the Egyptians on the battlefield. The Egyptians surrendered to the Persian army with little fight. This is the power of regrouping. The Persian army realized that in order to conquer an enemy, they had to be willing to try something different and be bold in their efforts. In the same way, we can't be afraid to learn from our past mistakes and try a new outlook and plan that will work for our family.

Whether you struggle with every battle or need to find peace due to a traumatic situation involving your child, if you want to stop these situations from controlling your life, you must be willing to allow the Lord to heal you and to try something new. Below are four crucial elements of regrouping.

Make a Choice to Accept Forgiveness

One step to healing in any situation is to make a choice to forgive. Often the message of the Bible is centralized on forgiving others (which we should always strive for). Yet when one has internalized guilt, he or she is the culprit and cause of the turmoil. I have found that it's far easier to forgive others than to forgive myself. The agony of my inner thoughts tormenting me about how I could have done better is often too much to bear. Here's the issue at hand: biblically, you will not find a verse on forgiving yourself. What you will find is that we serve a God who forgives. "If we confess our sins, he is faithful and just and will forgive us our sins and purify us from all unrighteousness" (1 John 1:9).

In other words, God sees past our mistakes and chooses to rid us from the condemnation. The One who has every right to point the finger chooses to forgive us. Our job is to stand in the place of acceptance of this free gift. In Him we can be set free from the heavy weight of regret that shackles us (Romans 8:1–2). What would our lives look like if we ran to the Lord and said, "Lord, I receive Your forgiveness and give You permission to heal me"? We serve a God who is more than capable of carrying our burdens and shame. All we need to do is seek Him. The Enemy will only be able to reign in this area of your life if you allow Him to. If you choose to remain bitter, you may become stuck in your own thoughts and unable to create a new way of doing things.

Develop an Accurate View of God

Our perception of who God is will play a role in how we regroup. If we see God as distant and unresponsive, we will carry the burden of every situation. We will assert that we should be in control of every matter. Yet if we see God as near and caring, we will know that He is not only with us as we heal, but He also stands alongside our children as they grow through the situations at hand. An accurate view of God sees Him as one who is all-knowing and who uses every situation for the good of His children (Romans 8:28). We can rest in the fact that God cares and loves our children more than we ever could. He has His eyes on our situation and is ready to give the instruction needed. Though we may be imperfect mothers learning as we go, nothing catches God off guard. Our job is to remember that He is the ultimate authority and to seek Him for the strategy needed.

Practice the Pause

When it comes to our motherhood, we must be willing to take the time to create a clear strategy for victory. As you are reading, consider pausing right now. Close your eyes and picture your ideal world as it pertains to parenting. How would your children behave? How would you respond to them? How would your children describe you as a parent? If you realized the Lord was observing you parent, how would you interact with your child?

In counseling, therapists will often use the ideal-world scenario to guide clients toward change. By taking time to consider what you want to see happen in your life, you can create clear goals and have a path toward victory. Within this scenario, we must also realize that (in most cases) we cannot change anyone else's behavior or thoughts. As mothers, however, we *can* recognize the ways we add to or take away from the home we desire to create. As we pause, we can ask the Lord to show us, *us*. "Search me, God, and know my heart; test me and know my anxious thoughts. See if there is any offensive way in me, and lead me in the way everlasting" (Psalm 139:23–24).

A crucial part of practicing the pause is to evaluate all aspects of the situation at hand. In doing so, we ask questions and think of every possible reason the situation may be happening and practical ways we can initiate change.

Let's practice the pause using the following scenario: a five-year-old who continues to have tantrums.

Questions to consider:

- Is the child getting enough rest?
- Is there a developmental issue?
- Has there been a consequence for tantrums?
- Are the consequences consistent?
- When do the tantrums happen the most and the least?
- When did the tantrums begin?

These questions can give insight to why the behavior is happening and how to end it. For this scenario, an earlier bedtime and clear consequences may solve the issue. Similarly, the child could be struggling with intense nightmares that require prayer and fasting or a change in what he watches on television. Keeping a journal to document the behavior can be a game changer and empower you to know how to make a change. However, if you are so busy being frustrated with the issue, you may never pause long enough to work toward a solution.

Initiate Change

Change is never easy but always necessary. In most cases, changes are best made one step at a time. Years ago I heard the story of a man who had become a senior pastor of an old, dilapidated church. In hopes of modernizing the church, the denomination hired a young pastor and tasked him to make a change. The first step: removing the organ from the stage and replacing it with a keyboard. He was aware that some of the older members would not be happy by this radical move. Rather than cause an uproar or church split, he came up with a plan: move the organ an inch every Sunday. One inch at a time, he moved the organ until after a few months the church didn't even notice that the organ had been removed. One small, intentional step at a time over an extended amount of time can lead to a significant change.

> **One small, intentional step at a time over an extended amount of time can lead to a significant change.**

In most cases, we can see the issue at hand and create steps toward the goal. In the example of the child who throws tantrums, the mother may be most successful if she tackles one area at a time. This method can be especially helpful when making changes in the lives of teenagers. Too much of a change at one time can lead to rebellion and resentment. It will also create more stress for you as you try to keep up and be consistent with your new rules and expectations. Nonetheless, for more serious matters, like dealing with a teen who continuously runs away from home or is caught indulging in risky behaviors like underage drinking or talking inappropriately to strangers online, regrouping may become a life-or-death situation. Changes may need to be vast, immediate, and without regard for anyone else's opinion. Don't be afraid to own your choices in these difficult matters. Though your child may not appreciate your choice now, he or she will thank you later.

As we end the chapter, I want to return to the story of Eve. After the death of Abel and casting away of Cain, Eve probably endured the heaviness of guilt in a way that many will never understand. Yet her words when she birthed Seth reveal her heart's condition in the moment. We read, "Adam made love to his wife again, and she gave birth to a son and named him Seth, saying, 'God has granted me another child in place of Abel, since Cain killed him'" (Genesis 4:25).

In this verse, the word *child*, or *seed*, is translated from the Hebrew word *zera*[3], denoting generations, offspring, and what happens before a harvest (Genesis 8:22). The word *zera* is different from the word *'iysh*, which Eve used at the birth of Cain. *'Iysh* simply means "man."[4] Thus, for Cain she celebrated the birth of one. Seth, however, she saw as seed for the many to follow. Eve's usage of the word *zera* implied a hope for the future. She made a choice not to dwell on what was lost but to see what God was going to do. Although she was aware of the pain from losing Cain and Abel, she believed the Lord for the harvest of generations to come. Instead of choosing guilt and pity, Eve chose to give God the glory. She chose to work through the pain and *parent on* with God on her side.

I encourage you to remember that although our parenting will be full of twists and turns, God's grace is sufficient. He can empower us with the wisdom to know how to navigate our parenthood and overcome the guilt that accompanies missing the mark. My prayer is that you make the choice to cast your burdens on the Lord and regroup, even when it's hard. If we rely on Him for our strength and to settle our souls, we will never be defeated.

───────────────── VICTORY VERSE ─────────────────

Give your burdens to the LORD, and he will take care of you. He will not permit the godly to slip and fall. (Psalm 55:22 NLT)

───────────────── REFLECTIONS ─────────────────

1. List the behavior(s) that your child displays that you could offer more grace for. What are ways in which you can help your child understand the consequences of his or her choices—in a way he or she can understand?
2. When it comes to being a mother, in what areas do you carry guilt?
3. What areas of your parenting require you to regroup? Create a list of a change you would like to make for each and one practical way you can get a step closer to this goal.

———————————————— POWER PRAYER ————————————————

Lord, I thank You for being with me every step of my parenting journey. Father, I need You to heal my heart. I surrender my past mistakes to You and ask that You forgive me. Forgive me for the words I have spoken and the actions I have taken that have caused harm to my children. Teach me, Lord, to run to You when I'm unsure of what to do. God, I look to You for strategy and wisdom in all things. You are my safe place. Thank You for accepting me in all my imperfection and for trusting me with Your beloved child. May my motherhood be a mighty testimony of Your goodness and grace. In Jesus's name. Amen.

Chapter Fifteen

THE HEART OF SERVICE

Live for something rather than die for nothing.
GENERAL GEORGE S. PATTON JR.

FROM THE BEGINNING OF TIME, people have fought wars. Wars over religion, territories, civil rights, and economic gain throughout human history would add up to an immeasurable amount of money. In the US alone, from the Revolutionary War until now, over 1.1 million people have been casualties of these perilous conflicts.[1] It's clear that many are willing to give their lives to stand up for what they believe. Many brave men and women have decided to be on the front lines of the world's toughest battles. Anyone can look at these soldiers, marines, sailors, and airmen and have a deep sense of respect for their mission. As a mother, you also serve in one of the most elite and essential services.

Warrior Mother, you've been appointed to the greatest mission on earth.

God has commissioned you to be on the front lines of His army. You have the privilege of serving and laying down your life, much like those in our military. This is no small feat or something to be overlooked—it is an honor. Other than Jesus Himself, you are the first line of defense against the Enemy's attacks. Your choices to nurture God's children, to train them up, and to direct them toward the Lord cannot be quantified by a dollar amount. You sacrifice your body through pregnancy and through the tireless nights of infancy. You give of your heart and your mind as you think of ways to make your child feel more loved in a world that constantly seeks to bring rejection. Cooking nourishing meals that will bring relief, setting up doctor's appointments, making choices about what's acceptable in your home, and praying from the depths of your soul are more than honorable. The very act of reading this book proves that you have a heart to serve, protect, and defend those you've been entrusted with.

Warrior Mother, you've been appointed to the greatest mission on earth—to mother your child in a way that reflects God's heart. When you commit to this mission and serve the Lord all your days, you will undoubtedly be greeted at heaven's gate with these words: "Well done, my good and faithful servant" (Matthew 25:23 NLT).

The Great Commission

Over the last fourteen chapters, we've journeyed through what it means to mother with God's heart. From the beauty of praying and fasting, to renewing our minds in Christ, to nurturing our children's giftings, mothering is not always an easy job. Yet all of this is a foundation laid for the most crucial opportunity in our parenting, to lead our children closer to the Lord. Your greatest mission as a mother is the Great Commission.

> Then Jesus came to them and said, "All authority in heaven and on earth has been given to me. Therefore go and make disciples of all nations, baptizing them in the name of the Father and of the Son and of the Holy Spirit, and teaching them to obey everything I have commanded you. And surely I am with you always, to the very end of the age." (Matthew 28:18–20)

Understanding the depth of Jesus's charge to His disciples is important. The word *commission* is an almost militant term and grants authority for a person to act. When one is commissioned in the government or military, she is given permission to act on behalf of her country or organization. When Jesus gave the command to make disciples, baptize, and teach new followers everything, this was more than a simple suggestion. Jesus was giving a direct military-style order for His followers to act accordingly and on His behalf. We can easily see that some of Jesus's last recorded words were a call to action. It wasn't enough for His disciples just to believe in Him— they also had to follow through and find more people to believe. The same is true for us today. Yes, God desires moms to be sold out for Him. But what's a bigger testimony is when mothers make a choice to replicate this passion for Christ within their own homes.

Jesus's commission to make disciples should be the heart of everything we do as mothers. Remembering that every action we take will draw our children toward God or away from Him, we should see our homes as mission fields. We get the privilege of teaching our children the Word, praying with them, and showing them what it means to live the gospel. In our homes we get to be a living, breathing testimony of what it means to live for Christ. What an honor! Motherhood may be tough, but it isn't a burden—it's an opportunity for God to use us in mighty ways.

Our society tends to convince us that our primary goals should be attaining wealth for the generations to come, creating memories, or helping our children be all they can be. Although these are great ideas, they must never be our primary goal. If we aren't careful, we can waste a lot of time worrying about what is perishable rather than what is eternal. I am constantly reminded of the verse that says, "What good is it for someone to gain the whole world, yet forfeit their soul?" (Mark 8:36). I ask you what would it profit you to have the most perfectly groomed children, more money than everyone you know, and the biggest house, while your children have no concept of who the Lord is? Wouldn't the eternal blessing of salvation far outweigh the temporal things of this world? Every time I think of this, I ask myself, *What more can I do, Lord? How else can I pray? What more can I do to show love?*

Our responsibility is to create the best opportunity to see our children fulfill all that God has called them to, including accepting Jesus as their Savior. This is my why! This is my why for all that I do.

This is why I'm willing to cry out to the Lord for their souls.

This is why I will pray and fast to see a breakthrough in my home.

This is why, I'm willing to teach them the Word.

This is why I'm willing to bring correction.

This is why I make the choice to be emotionally available when I want to check out.

The Great Commission is the living and active reason for all aspects of my life and parenting journey. It remains my firm foundation as I interact with the world around me and as I mother. If you also make this your highest goal, you will see that most of your decisions regarding your parenting will be an easy yes or no. In fact, you will rule out anything that might hinder you from winning souls and making disciples. And although it may require removing certain habits, praying against certain strongholds, or changing up some relationships to get there, I have no doubt you can do this. You can go from being a defeated victim of life to being a defender of the gospel within your home. So I implore you not to fall into the trap of perfectionism by trying to implement overnight every aspect you've learned in this book. Remember that taking one intentional small step at a time will lead to significant change. Each week is a new opportunity for a new goal to be enacted in your home. This is how we fight strategically.

To the Brokenhearted

I want to take a moment to talk to those who feel like you've done all that you can to lead your children to the Lord, only to be disappointed. Perhaps the child who grew up in church is now an atheist. Maybe your child has become trapped in addiction or has another vice that has caused him to walk away from the Lord. Perhaps your child was hurt badly by someone in the church, and it seems impossible to win her back to the Lord. Or maybe you are just coming to the Lord and feel like it's too late to influence your older children to know Him. Warrior Mother, there is still hope!

God is a good Father and desires that none of His children should perish (2 Peter 3:9). So although you may feel helpless, know that we serve a God who cares and will continue to draw them to Himself. But while you wait for them to accept or return to the Lord, don't you dare stop warring on their behalf in continual prayer! Don't even consider changing how deep you love them even if they are far in distance or running away from God. If your son or daughter chooses to reject you, love them more from a distance. One thing I have learned while training future counselors is this: we cannot change anyone's behavior—all we can do is provide information. Share the gospel as you can, love hard, and allow the Holy Spirit to do the work as only He can. I am drawn to what Paul said to the Corinthian church. "I planted the seed, Apollos watered it, but God has been making it grow" (1 Corinthians 3:6).

In other words, we have to trust in God's process for our children's lives. We may be the ones who planted the seed of the gospel. God may send a coworker or a spouse to water the seed. Like a natural plant, it may take a few seasons to see the seed blossom into the fullness of what it's called to be. But it is the Lord who will make it grow. It is the work of the Holy Spirit to bring revelation and help our kids have an encounter where they finally accept Jesus as their Lord. From personal experience, I can say that it's an entirely different experience when you come to the Lord after He touches you personally rather than from salvation just being taught to you from infancy. I've found that those with a radical testimony of God saving them in adulthood enter the Christian faith fired up and ready to serve Him. I believe it's because they've tried everything else in the world only to find that God is the answer to every issue and every circumstance.

Let us not grow weary in praying for God to have a supernatural encounter with our children even now. Amen!

As long as they have breath in their bodies, God can still save their souls. We see this clearly when Jesus was on the cross beside the believing thief. Instead of looking down on him for his life of poor choices, Jesus gave him a final chance by saying, "Truly I tell you, today you will be with me in paradise" (Luke 23:43). Yes, the Lord is willing to forgive anyone who has the heart to believe in Him. Stay in hope that your child can turn around at any time and that the Lord will embrace him or her with open arms. This is the beautiful message of the cross—that while we were still sinners, Christ saved us. He can do the same for your child today.

The Good Shepherd

As we take this giant leap into parenting in a new way, remember that you serve a God who is present. The Bible calls Him our Good Shepherd. As mentioned in chapter 9, a shepherd doesn't take his job lightly. A shepherd is intentional and goes to great lengths to protect his flock and lead the sheep to their destination. So much so that a good shepherd will leave the entire flock to go after one that is missing. This is why Jesus spoke of the great joy when one person comes to Christ, even more than over the ninety-nine who never left. You see, we serve a God whose love for us and for our children is so vast that He is willing to do anything to get to us and save us—including giving His life for us. This is what a great shepherd does. Psalm 23 says it like this:

> The Lord is my shepherd, I lack nothing.
> He makes me lie down in green pastures,
> he leads me beside quiet waters,
>   he refreshes my soul.
> He guides me along the rights paths
>   for his name's sake.

Even though I walk
　　through the darkest valley,
I will fear no evil,
　　for you are with me;
your rod and your staff,
　　they comfort me.

You prepare a table before me
　　in the presence of my enemies.
You anoint my head with oil;
　　my cup overflows.
Surely your goodness and love will follow me
　　all the days of my life,
and I will dwell in the house of the LORD
　　forever.

What amazing promises we find in this passage from our Good Shepherd!

- He gives you rest.
- He refreshes your soul.
- He places you on the right path.
- He walks with you through the toughest moments.
- He gives you peace in the toughest moments.
- He comforts you, even in the correction.
- He blesses you, even in front of those who think you don't deserve it.
- He anoints you to do what He's called you to do and protects you from the irritations of life.[2]
- His goodness and love are always with you.

If you take to heart no other Scripture in this book, my prayer is that Psalm 23 becomes your reality. In this chapter God is reminding us that we don't have to live life or mother from a place of weariness.

Just like a shepherd to a sheep, the Lord has placed the burden on Himself to care for us. Instead of carrying the weight of motherhood all alone, we can rely fully on Christ to lead us and our children. If we can lean into this, many of our sleepless nights will be replaced with times of prayer. Our times of worrying will give way to remembering all that God has done. Our fears will be a reminder of our need to trust God more. When we completely surrender our parenting journey to Him, though we will face tough times, we will find security and peace in Him.

Marching into Victory

Warrior Mother, I want to leave you with some final marching orders straight from the US military. One thing I noticed during my husband's time in active duty was the popular mottoes of each branch. These mottoes are the heartbeat of their missions, and each one can also give *you* something to hold to during the woes and triumphs of motherhood. I proclaim the following phrases over your parenting journey.

- *Semper fi. Always faithful.* I encourage you to always be faithful like the marines. Commit to motherhood with all your heart, soul, and strength. Be faithful in love, in perseverance, and by making the choice to show up when no one else does.
- *This we'll defend.* Like the US Army, let us make the choice to defend our children in life's battles. May we defend in everyday battles when we feel they are being treated poorly. May we defend in spiritual matters as we pray for protection from every attack of the Enemy. Defend in prayer. Defend in action.
- *Semper fortis. Always courageous.* This unofficial motto of the navy is your reminder to be brave during every trial. Even when you feel like you've given it all that you can, push on just a little more. Give it one more try. As you walk in courage, you empower your child to do the same. Remember, God is with you in every battle and will never leave you or forsake you.

- *Aim high . . . Fly-fight-win.* It's no surprise that the US Air Force encourages its airmen to fly high. Let's use this call-and-response motto to encourage us to take our parenting to the next level. May we never become complacent with how things have been. No matter how great things are, we can always grow, learn, and change for the better. Imagine God's best for your life and be willing to go for it. Refuse to allow any lie of the Enemy, your past sins, or insecurity to keep you from being the mother God has called you to be.

- *Semper supra. Always above.* The youngest military branch, the US Space Force, inspires us to operate in excellence. In everything we do, let us seek to go above and beyond. Let's set the standard high for what it means to serve Christ by living a life that honors Him. Let us be the loudest cheerleaders for our children and the ones who will pray for them when no one else will. Even more so, let us keep our mind on the promises from heaven above. May God's perspective be our vantage point. May we remember that we are above, not beneath. The head, not the tail. Victorious, not victims.

- *Semper paratus. Always ready.* Last but not least, I implore you with the words of the brave Coasties who protect the seas. *Always* be ready! Rather than await the next storm of life to come, prepare now. Put on your spiritual armor and keep it on at all times so that you can stand against every ploy of the Enemy. Gird yourself with truth, righteousness, faith, peace, the message of the cross, and the Word. Never find yourself in a battle unprepared, but remain always mindful of your spiritual condition. It will be hard to fight for your child's spiritual gains when you are wounded yourself.

Thank you for taking this journey with me. As a mom of seven, I am still ever learning how much God cares about our parenting journeys. My prayer is that God has opened the eyes of your heart to see Him and know Him better. I have no doubt that you will see God move radically in your parenting if you're willing. If we keep our eyes focused on sharing God's love to children, we can never go wrong. Let us keep our prayers focused, spiritual armor ready, and devotion to the greatest mission on earth—mothering God's children. Stay faithful and watch as the Lord moves you from

Defeated to defender,
Fearful to fearless,
Victim to victor,
Worrier to warrior.

"'Not by might nor by power, but by my Spirit,' says the Lord Almighty" (Zechariah 4:6).

——————————— VICTORY VERSE ———————————

I have no greater joy than to hear that my children are walking in the truth. (3 John 1:4)

——————————— REFLECTIONS ———————————

1. List practical ways you can share the gospel in your home. Seek to implement one each week.
2. Which promise of the Good Shepherd brings you the most encouragement? How have you seen this in your parenting so far?
3. Which military motto speaks to your heart the most? Which one is a struggle for you?
4. What are you believing for most in your parenting? Find a biblical story or promise of the Lord you can lean into to encourage you in this.

——————————— POWER PRAYER ———————————

Lord, I thank You for _____. Each of my children is a special gift from You. Help me never to take this opportunity to mother them for granted. Lord, let me never forget to share the message of the gospel. May every choice I make be filtered through You. Teach me to share Your Word in a practical way. Bring Your conviction when my actions cause a distraction for my children. Lord, I ask for Your help in running with this mission. Teach me to be faithful when times are difficult. Show me how to defend the gospel when the world brings a contradicting message. Help me to be courageous and remember that You are always with me. Guide me down the path of righteousness, and show me how to always operate from the heavenly realm. Lord, teach me to operate with excellence and commit wholeheartedly to every aspect of parenting. Show me how to love my children the way You would call me to. And, Lord, help me to always be ready for every spiritual attack. When I feel weak, remind me that I am strong with You. Help me to war in the spirit from the depth of my soul. I trust You, Lord. I completely surrender to You, my Commander, my Savior, and my Father. In Jesus's name. Amen.

"The Lord gives the command; the women who proclaim good news are a great army" (Psalm 68:11 NASB).

Acknowledgments

WITH MY SINCEREST LOVE AND appreciation, I acknowledge:

My husband, Joseph: I will never regret saying "I do" to you. Not only did you introduce me to what it means to serve the Lord wholeheartedly, but you allow me to blossom and encourage me to live out God's call for my life. I thank you for giving me seven amazing gifts—our children.

My children, Trinity, Joey, Christian, Isaiah, David, Heavenly Joy, and Malachi: You teach me so much. Every day with you is a new opportunity to learn, grow, and love like I could never imagine. Each of you is my favorite and my greatest joy.

My mother, Angela: Your encouragement has kept me over the years. I thank you for being more than a parent—a friend. I pray to be a mother of such resilience, courage, and honor, like you.

My father, Reggie: Your support has shown me that true parenting has nothing to do with biology but everything to do with heart. Your genuine care and support remind me that love has no boundaries.

My sister, Diamond: Your tenacity and inner strength give me courage. I'm inspired by your heart and determination to do all that God has called you to do, while being an amazing mother.

My God-given family, Enlighten Church: I thank you for the prayers that gave me hope to keep going when I wanted to give up. Your enthusiasm to see me live out God's vision has not gone unseen. It's an honor to serve alongside you in ministry.

My literary agent, Blythe: I thank you for seeing the vision of this book and for taking a chance on me. I appreciate how you have upheld this project with care, love, and genuine support.

My unofficial coach, Megan Elizabeth Brown: Your excitement to share God's Word is contagious. Thank you for being an integral part of my journey and for the work you do for so many military spouses.

My prayer supporters and mentors, Tammy, Mama Lee, Audrey B, and the countless others: I say thank you for seeing the best in me and being a safe place for me to share my heart. I praise God for you.

My Kregel Publications team: Your heart to see mothers walk in victory and your willingness to stand behind this project continually keep me humbled. Thank you for the countless hours invested and the excellence that you've brought along the way.

Suggested Books

- *1-2-3 Magic: The New 3-Step Discipline for Calm, Effective, and Happy Parenting* by Thomas Phelan
- *The 5 Love Languages of Children: The Secret to Loving Children Effectively* by Gary Chapman
- *The Bible Made Easy—for Kids* by Dave Strehler
- *The Family Bible Devotional: Stories from the Bible to Help Kids and Parents Engage and Love Scripture* by Sarah Wells
- *Heaven Is for Real for Kids: A Little Boy's Astounding Story of His Trip to Heaven and Back* by Todd Burpo
- *NIV Mom's Devotional Bible* by Elisa Morgan
- *The One Year Praying through the Bible for Your Kids* by Nancy Guthrie
- *Sparkling Gems from the Greek Vol. 1: 365 Greek Word Studies for Every Day of The Year to Sharpen Your Understanding of God's Word* by Rick Renner
- *Unmasking the Devil: Strategies to Defeat Eternity's Greatest Enemy* by John Ramirez

Notes

Chapter One: Unleash the Warrior

1. Stephen Coonts, *The Art of War* (New York: St. Martin's Paperbacks, 2017), 14.
2. Peg Streep, "7 Common Wounds for Daughters of Unloving Mothers," *Psychology Today*, April 30, 2013, https://www.psychologytoday.com/us/blog/tech-support/201304/7-common-wounds-daughters-unloving-mothers.
3. Jon Harper, "Cost of Post–9/11 Wars Expected to Top $6 trillion," National Defense, December 24, 2019, https://www.nationaldefensemagazine.org/articles/2019/12/24/cost-of-post-911-wars-expected-to-top-6-trillion.

Chapter Two: Know Your Place

1. Mary J. England and Leslie J. Sim, eds., *Depression in Parents, Parenting, and Children* (Washington, DC: National Academies Press, 2009), summary, from the NCBI bookshelf, https://www.ncbi.nlm.nih.gov/books/NBK215117/.

Chapter Four: Oath to Love

1. Carl E. Pickhardt, "Adolescence and the Management of Parental Love," *Psychology Today*, May 21, 2012, https://www.psychologytoday.com/us/blog/surviving-your-childs-adolescence/201205/adolescence-and-the-management-parental-love.
2. Jim Taylor, "Three Ways to Raise Secure Children," *Psychology Today*, January 23, 2014, https://www.psychologytoday.com/us/blog/the-power-prime/201401/three-ways-raise-secure-children.

3. "Oath of Enlistment," US Army, accessed July 15, 2021, https://www.army.mil/values/oath.html.

Chapter Five: Victory Minded
1. David Myers and C. Nathan DeWall, "The Biology of Behavior," in *Exploring Psychology* (New York: Worth, Macmillan Learning, 2016), 60–61.
2. Elizabeth Pratt, "Negative Thinking Can Harm Your Brain and Increase Your Dementia Risk," *Healthline*, June 11, 2020, https://www.healthline.com/health-news/negative-thinking -can-harm-brain-increase-dementia-risk#How-to-be-more -positive.

Chapter Six: Squared Away
1. Robert J. Hedaya, *Understanding Biological Psychiatry* (New York: W. W. Norton, 1996), 189–200.

Chapter Seven: War of Deception
1. John Ramirez, *Unmasking the Devil: Strategies to Defeat Eternity's Greatest Enemy* (Shippensburg, PA: Destiny Image, 2015), 17.
2. Tony Evans, "Using Prayer to Overcome Spiritual Warfare," November 17, 2019, YouTube video, 14:23, https://www.you tube.com/watch?v=Z5a0WHXOG6c.
3. "Nazi Propaganda," Holocaust Encyclopedia, accessed February 10, 2022, https://encyclopedia.ushmm.org/content/en /article/nazi-propaganda?series=1.
4. "A Revealing Experiment: Brown v. Board and the 'Doll Test,'" NAACP Legal Defense and Educational Fund, accessed July 21, 2021, https://www.naacpldf.org/ldf-celebrates-60th-anniversa ry-brown-v-board-education/significance-doll-test.

Chapter Eight: Strategic Prayer
1. Lance Wallnau, "Breaking Off Familiar Spirits," *Lance Wall-*

nau (blog), accessed February 11, 2022, https://lancewallnau
.com/breaking-off-familiar-spirits/.

Chapter Nine: Modeling the Faith

1. Douglas Bernstein, *Psychology: Foundations and Frontiers*, 10th ed. (Boston: Cengage, 2016), 717.
2. Alina-Mihaela Buşan, "Learning Styles of Medical Students: Implications in Education," *Current Health Sciences Journal* 40, no. 2 (April–June 2014): 104–10, https://www.ncbi.nlm .nih.gov/pmc/articles/PMC4340450.
3. Albert Bandura, *Social Foundations of Thought and Action: A Social Cognitive Theory* (Englewood Cliffs, NJ: Prentice Hall, 1986), 21.
4. Christopher J. Ferguson, "Did the Bobo Doll Studies Teach Us About Aggression?," *Psychology Today*, March 21, 2020, https://www.psychologytoday.com/us/blog/checkpoints /202003/did-the-bobo-doll-studies-teach-us-about-aggresion.

Chapter Ten: Train Them Up

1. "H2596—Ḥānak—Strong's Hebrew Lexicon (NIV)," Blue Letter Bible, accessed July 26, 2022, https://www.blueletterbible .org/lexicon/h2596/niv/wlc/0-1/.
2. Diana Baumrind, "Effects of Authoritative Parental Control on Child Behavior," *Child Development* 37, no. 4 (December 1966): 887–907, https://www.jstor.org/stable/1126611?origin =crossref.
3. E. E. Maccoby and J. A. Martin, "Socialization in the Context of the Family: Parent-Child Interaction," in *Handbook of Child Psychology, Volume IV: Socialization, Personality and Social Development*, ed. Paul H. Mussen and E. Mavis Hetherington, 4th ed. (New York: Wiley, 1983).
4. Tracy Trautner, "Authoritative Parenting Style," Michigan State University Extension, January 19, 2017, https://www .canr.msu.edu/news/authoritative_parenting_style.

5. Daniel Huerta, "Is Spanking Biblical?," Focus on the Family, 2018, https://www.focusonthefamily.com/parenting/is-spank ing-biblical.

Chapter Eleven: Morale Matters

1. Dan Garisto, "New Smoke Alarm Tests a Mother's Touch," *Science News Explores*, December 11, 2018, https://www.science newsforstudents.org/article/moms-voice-is-best-fire-alarm.

Chapter Twelve: Unexpected Explosions

1. BibleHub, Strong's Concordance, s.v. "sovereignty," accessed July 5, 2022, https://biblehub.com/greek/932.htm.

Chapter Thirteen: Battle Buddies

1. "Military 'Battle Buddy' System Comes to Hospitals and Clinics," University of Minnesota, May 5, 2020, https://twin -cities.umn.edu/news-events/military-battle-buddy-system -comes-hospitals-and-clinics.
2. BibleHub, Matthew Poole's Commentary, "Proverbs 27:17," accessed February 7, 2022 https://biblehub.com/commentaries /proverbs/27-17.htm.

Chapter Fourteen: The Power of Regrouping

1. Scott Floyd, *Crisis Counseling: A Guide for Pastors and Professionals* (Grand Rapids: Kregel Academic, 2008), 24.
2. Michael Hotchkiss, "Weighed Down by Guilt: Research Shows It's More Than a Metaphor," Princeton University, October 8, 2013, https://www.princeton.edu/news/2013/10/08/weighed -down-guilt-research-shows-its-more-metaphor.
3. "H2233—zera'—Strong's Hebrew Lexicon (KJV)," Blue Letter Bible, accessed December 9, 2022, https://www.blueletterbible .org/lexicon/h2233/kjv/wlc/0-1/.
4. "H376—'îš—Strong's Hebrew Lexicon (NIV)," Blue Letter

Bible, accessed December 9, 2022, https://www.blueletterbible .org/lexicon/h376/niv/wlc/0-1/.

Chapter Fifteen: The Heart of Service

1. Megan Crigger and Laura Santhanam, "How Many Americans Have Died in U.S. Wars?," PBS News Hour, May 24, 2015, https://www.pbs.org/newshour/nation/many-americans-died -u-s-wars.
2. Oil is often placed on a sheep's head to protect it from flies and from developing certain skin diseases.

About the Author

VICTORIA RIOLLANO IS A MILITARY mom of seven who holds an MA in child and adolescent psychology. She is a professor of psychology at three universities as well as a co-pastor and church planter with her husband. She is also the singer of "My Victory," available on all music platforms. Her writing has previously been featured on Crosswalk, iBelieve, the YouVersion Bible app, and *Christianity Today.* Learn more about Victoria and find inspiration on how you can win in every area of your life at victoryspeaks.org.